Hey, Lord, Can Angels Type?

Hey, Lord, Can Angels Type?

5-Minute Devotions for Working Women

Faye Roberts

SAINT LOUIS

2   3   4   5   6   7   8   9 10   05   04   03   02   01   00   99   98   97   96

This book is dedicated to the many women whose honesty, perseverance, humor, and hard work gave me the inspiration to finish what I started.

To my husband, Tom, for going to bed many nights without me.

To my sons, Chris and Todd, who have learned to run the washing machine.

To my daughters, Amy and Mandy, for allowing me to grow up beside them.

To Judy and Debbie, who spent a lot of lunch hours encouraging me when I was ready to quit.

And to Tom and Darrell at the bank for working with me and giving me the time needed to achieve my dream.

Thanks to all of you.

Table of

Contents

Comfort Me, Mom • The Ant • Chocolate Chip
Bran Muffins • Opening the Door • Take a Hike,
Jane Fonda! • Spring Cleaning • Prairie Dog •
Lunch with the Girls • A Time to Weep • Grant
Me Patience, Now! • The Failure • Hide-and-Seek
• Falling Together • Charge It • The Fire • I Am
Not a Quitter! • The Dinner Party • Die ... it! •
An Imperfect Christian • The Cat in the Hat •
Bless Me with Wings • The Reunion • Working
Late • The Healing Touch • A Little Soap and
Water • Fired Up • Get It in Gear!

Section 6: Life Savors

Penguins and Platypuses • A Voice in the Stillness
• The Bread of Human Kindness • The Fountain
Pen • Coasting • Old Things • Love Letters •
Angel Windows • The Tattered Old Bible • Turn-
ing 40 • My Secret Garden • Betty • Monday
Blues • The Road Less Traveled • Fasting •
Cleaning House • The Bag Lady in Burger King •
All That Really Matters • Looking Back

SECTION 1

GOD GOT A DAY OFF, WHY DON'T I?

Can Angels Type?

The angel of the Lord encamps around
those who fear Him, and He delivers them.
Psalm 34:7

Don't get me wrong, Lord. I'm grateful for the angels watching over me. I know they've put in a lot of overtime this year.

But the ringing phone needs to be answered, and I've got to get this report finished. There are six phone messages that need prompt attention. One is from my son, who's home sick with the stomach flu, and I feel guilty about not being there.

I've misplaced the dictionary and can't remember how to spell *effecient*. Isn't there another *i* in there somewhere? I have a run in my pantyhose. These high heels are crushing my toes. The copy machine is jammed. I can't figure out how to add the toner. My chair squeaks every time I move. And the piped-in music is playing the same tape for the 44th time.

The customer on the other side of my cluttered desk is complaining about his bill and the person I need to talk to about the problem is on voice mail. I try another number and get put on hold. At least the music is different.

Hey, Lord, can angels type?

Prayer

Lord, when the problems come fast and furious, and I feel as though You are far away, help me see Your angels watching over me. Give me the strength to set my priorities and finish my jobs. Give me trust in Your timing—the scheduling that sent Your Son to be my Savior at the right time. In Jesus' name. Amen.

The Working Woman

She considers a field and buys it; out of
her earnings she plants a vineyard.
Proverbs 31:16

It's comforting to know that the virtuous woman described in Proverbs was actually a businesswoman.

As I read the description of the noble lady, she was not much different than the working woman of today. She worked with eager hands. She set about her work vigorously. Her trading was profitable. She was an entrepreneur.

She was also a mother. She got up early, while it was still dark, to provide food for her family. She made sure her family was warmly clothed when cold weather threatened. I'm sure she must have stood by the door and reminded her little ones not to forget their hats as she handed out lunches.

The woman was a supportive wife, bringing her husband good, not harm, all the days of her life. Her husband admired her hard-working spirit.

I wonder if this ancient woman felt guilty about not being home with her family as she tended her vineyards. I wonder if she sometimes felt overwhelmed because too many people needed her. She probably prayed for a few minutes of peace and quiet.

This virtuous woman must have found a certain joy in earning her way and welcoming the challenges in her life. One of the most interesting parts about the woman described in Proverbs was her ability to laugh. "She is clothed with strength and dignity; she can laugh at the days to come" (31:25). Just knowing that she laughed makes me feel like that woman is my sister, even though we were born more than 2,000 years apart.

But what finally sets this woman apart and brings her praise? The writer says "a woman who fears the Lord is to be praised" (v. 30). The virtuous woman's faith in the Lord brings her the reward and the respect of her fellow townspeople. She and I can afford to laugh—we have the same God who holds us up and strengthens us to meet all our challenges.

Prayer

Dearest God, as I strive to become more like the noble woman described in Proverbs, help me remember that even now charm is deceptive and beauty is fleeting. Help me to be the kind of mother whose children think of her as a blessing. Remind me that—through Your guidance and the redeeming work of Jesus—I can laugh at the days ahead. And most of all, send Your Spirit to strengthen my faith so that I can be a witness to others. In Jesus' name. Amen.

Looking Forward to the Weekend

So on the seventh day He rested from all His work. *Genesis 2:2*

Am I looking forward to the weekend? What do you think? I have serious grocery shopping to do. The spiders have been partying for a month in the corners. The dog needs a bath. The bills need to be paid. The car needs to be washed. The library books are overdue. I'm afraid to look under the boys' beds, and I can't even find the laundry room.

After a full week of work ... I need rest!

I'll give myself a facial and get my nails done. I'll have breakfast in bed and read that novel I bought two months ago. Maybe my husband and I will go on a picnic, just the two of us, with a basket of wine and cheese.

On Sunday, we'll go to church and take the kids out to lunch. We'll stop at the park and fly a kite. And on the way home, we can get ice cream.

Oh, yes! I'm really looking forward to the weekend!

Prayer

Lord, You have the right idea. Help me put work and rest in the right perspective. If You took time to rest after Your work week, so should I. Provide me with the opportunities to enjoy the family You have given me. Help me relax in the world You have created. Above all, help me set aside time to worship You. Recharge my spiritual batteries for the week ahead. In Jesus' name. Amen.

The Performance Appraisal

This is to My Father's glory, that you bear much fruit. *John 15:8*

I left my new supervisor's office in anger, blinking back the tears. I crammed the performance appraisal in my desk drawer and slammed it shut.

It isn't fair! I have been with the company for 10 years. I work hard. I come in early and stay late. Last year, my old boss gave me an "excellent" rating along with a hefty raise. My new boss says my work is "average." Now my raise will be the same—average.

Well, no more! No more going the extra mile for the customers or for my new boss. I'll do my job. That's it. No more. No less.

I was still fuming when an elderly woman approached my desk. Her husband had recently died. She was confused by all the paperwork. I straightened out her accounts. That was my job.

The woman was still confused.

There was a time when I had been a widow too. I explained her Social Security benefits and helped her with the insurance forms. She was at my desk for almost an hour. As she rose to leave, she blinked a few times, just as I had done an hour ago. Then she gave me a hug.

"Thank you, dear. You have been a godsend."

After the woman left, I thought about those words. I reached in my desk drawer, pulled out the performance appraisal, and threw it in the shredder.

Prayer

Lord, I know You are my real supervisor. You're the only boss I ever really have to answer to. Don't ever let me settle for "average." Help me strive to be the best in all that I do. Then my light will shine out. And You will receive the praise as those around me view me as a "Godsend." In Jesus' name. Amen.

Too Many Bosses

Whenever I bring clouds over the earth and the rainbow appears in the clouds, I will remember My covenant between Me and you and all living creatures of every kind. *Genesis 9:14–15*

The instructor at the banking production seminar advises us, yet again, to treat every customer as if that person were our boss.

"Give them what they want," he firmly adds.

One banker yawns. Another doodles grocery

items on the note section of the handout. "What we really need is less time spent on sales meetings so we can get some work done," a co-worker whispers, and we chuckle in agreement. The instructor chides us with a science-teacher glare.

I pull the organizer from my briefcase, the latest attempt to put some order in my junk-drawer lifestyle. The Thursday to-do list grimly reminds me I already have more bosses than I can handle. After eight hours at my "real" job, I have to pay bills, find volleyball knee pads for my daughter, pick up a birthday present, bake cupcakes for school tomorrow, and have dinner with my husband. We have agreed to a date once a month.

A black cloud of stress begins to build as I secretly hope for a message that says my "date" will have to work late. It's hard to feel romantic from 7:30 p.m. until 9 p.m., knowing there are cupcakes to frost and laundry to fold.

It's only 3 p.m., and I'm already beat. The cloud looms closer as I wonder if I'm anemic.

During the coffee break, I make a courageous attempt to stick to the schedule in the organizer. I call the bakery to order cupcakes.

"How much?" I gasp. "$13.50," comes the bored reply.

"For cupcakes?" I repeat. "Fifty cents each, ma'am," the detached voice confirms.

The cloud of stress darkens. I could make them for $3, but I order them anyway and place another call.

The instructor begins speaking while I'm on hold with the sporting goods store. Finally, the voice interrupts the canned music to inform me the knee pads have been back ordered.

"But she needs them for Saturday night," I protest. "Sorry, ma'am," another bored voice answers.

The cloud of stress turns from gray to black, and I feel a drop of rain. My supervisor's eyes flash lightening bolts at me as I slip into my seat in time to hear the instructor explain how important it is to follow the guidelines he just gave on the new IRS regulations.

"Mrs. Roberts, would you like to explain the new interest calculation for retirement bonds?"

My mouth is bone dry even though the rain is now pelting down in sheets.

And I've forgotten my umbrella.

Prayer

Lord, I just can't answer to all these bosses in my life. I can't always give everyone what they want. Shelter me from the deluge of requests. As I peek out from beneath the protection of Your umbrella, please, show me Your rainbow. Help me see You by my side, ready, willing, and able to give me the strength to live my life by Your priorities. In Jesus' name. Amen.

Eating Bitter Words

The words of a gossip are like choice morsels. *Proverbs 18:8*

I was drawn in at coffee break. My unkind words about our co-worker added to the stew of sarcasm. We had quite a feast at the woman's expense.

She is hard to get along with at times, but I had no right to talk about her.

I know better, having once been on the receiving end of gossip. Someone thought I couldn't hear the slander spoken against me—but I did. I hid in the bathroom and wiped my eyes with coarse toilet paper. I will never forget the cruel words that slashed like a dull, jagged knife.

Now I've done the same wrong to another.

Once spoken, the tasty morsels of gossip quickly turn rancid.

Now I choke on my bitter words.

Prayer

Lord, guard my tongue when I'm tempted to talk behind someone's back. Bring to mind Your command against false testimony. When I do take part in the feast of gossip, point my eyes to Jesus, who died so that I might be forgiven. In His name. Amen.

The Woman in White Linen

Do not judge. *Matthew 7:1*

I instantly regretted offering to serve on the committee with the woman in the white linen suit. She looked like she'd just stepped out of the pages of *Vogue,* not a hair out of place. Her tailored clothes were understated yet very classy. Her shoes and handbag matched perfectly, and a tasteful bracelet glistened on her arm. She was fashionably thin, the owner and president of a very impressive company.

I wore jeans and discount store tennis shoes.

She asked me to meet on Saturday to discuss plans.

"Do you mind if we have lunch at my house? I'm expecting an important phone call."

"That's fine," I stammered. The woman made me nervous.

Even on a Saturday she looked terrific in her white slacks and turquoise silk shirt. The house was tasteful yet understated.

"Shall we sit in the library? I'll have Martha serve lunch while we go over the agenda."

The room was surprisingly cozy. Her desk was antique mahogany and on top was a gold frame with a picture of a boy and a handsome man inside.

"Your family?" I asked.

"Why, yes." She didn't offer any more information.

We dined on cucumber sandwiches and iced tea with limes. No wonder she was so thin, I thought. The phone rang. She almost knocked her glass over trying to answer it.

"Davey? Now, honey. You know I can't bring you home. I promise I will see you this afternoon. I love you too."

The woman quietly replaced the receiver, discreetly turned away and dabbed her eyes with an embroidered hankie. "I'm sorry, but could we finish this meeting later next week? I will have Martha see you out." She turned and quickly left the room.

"Please excuse her, ma'am. Today's her son's birthday, and she's sorry he can't be with her," Martha explained as she walked me out.

What a coldhearted woman, I thought. Probably has him conveniently tucked away in some boarding school. Martha read my mind and continued.

"Ten years ago her husband and son were hit by a drunk driver. Her husband died instantly, and Davey sustained massive head injuries. He needs special care. She tried to take care of him herself. She even quit her job and started a computer business out of her home. When she found a school that could teach Davey what she never could, she did the right thing and let him go. It broke her heart when he left.

"She threw herself into the only thing she had left—her work. Now she has a million-dollar business, but she would give it all up to have that one day back, 10 years ago."

On Monday I sent the woman a classy, yet understated, bouquet of flowers thanking her for lunch. I hope the beautiful woman and I can become friends.

Prayer

Lord, help me never categorize another human being. Forgive my childish jealousy and open my eyes—and my heart—to all people, Jesus, whether they're wearing silk, rags, or even discount store tennis shoes. In Your name. Amen.

Burned-Out

You, O Lord, keep my lamp burning;
my God turns my darkness into light.
Psalm 18:28

I'm burned-out. This job no longer fascinates me. What used to be interesting is now tedious. What was once intriguing is now monotonous.

It's a chore to get to work in the morning. I'm stuck in an another-day-another-dollar routine, and my rut grows deeper and deeper. The hands on the clock seem to move more slowly; even a fresh battery doesn't help.

I gaze out the window and get jealous of the hot dog vendor on the corner. At least he works for himself and not some major corporation. He doesn't punch a time clock or wonder if the supervisor is watching. He smiles at his customers.

Ho-hum drum ... What changed? Was it the job

or me? What did I do differently?

I learned. Every day brought new challenges that forced my brain to work. Now work has become repetitious. Should I move on? Climb new mountains? Or is there something left for me here? We do have a great insurance plan. And the people I work with are like family.

I'll talk to my supervisor. I want to do more. I want to learn and grow and achieve. I don't want to become stagnant. I need fresh ideas bubbling through me.

I don't want to slowly disintegrate inside, Lord. I don't want to spend one-third of my working life just getting by. I want to go for the glory, press on toward the goal, feel useful and vibrant. Give me the strength and wisdom to get out of this bleak, boring rut.

I know that if I show my boss I'm willing to tackle bigger projects, he'll respect my ambition. And if he doesn't, then I'll start looking to new horizons. Maybe I'll take a class, volunteer at a shelter, or become a partner to a troubled teen. Maybe I can ask for a different position or start an exercise program or …

Prayer

Lord, thank You for Your guiding hand. Thank You for this vibrant, adventurous feeling. Help me find ways to use my energy for Your good. Continue to fuel my enthusiasm so it will burn brightly and not burn out. In Jesus' name. Amen.

An Important Phone Call

Before they call I will answer; while they are still speaking I will hear. *Isaiah 65:24*

"Are there phones in heaven, Lord?" Just a minute, I have to put you on hold ...

"Do the lines ring constantly?" One moment, please ...

"Do people interrupt when You are dealing with the world's many problems?" For information on famine, press 1 ...

"At least You don't get transferred to a different department." For financial information, press 2 ...

"And I've never had to deal with call waiting when I talk to You." Please leave your message on voice mail ...

"It's nice to know that the call will always go through." I'm sorry, the number you are trying to reach is no longer in service ...

"Lord, thank You for not putting me on hold, especially when it's urgent."

Prayer

Thank You, dear Father, for giving me the number for Your direct line. Thank You for never putting me on hold. Thank You for promising always to answer my calls for help. Give me Your Holy Spirit's guidance to listen for Your answers. Thank You for the free gift of faith, which allows me to ask that Your will be done. In the name of Jesus, who taught me to pray. Amen.

Give Me a Break!

After [Jesus] had dismissed them, He went up on a mountainside by Himself to pray.
Matthew 14:23

Thank You, Lord, for this small break in my day. I can take a brisk walk around the block, stretch my knotted muscles, and spend a few moments of quiet time with You.

Thank You for listening as I try to reorganize my cluttered mind. It's almost as bad as my desk. I need these few moments to sort and file the immense amount of information that has piled up. I need to evaluate my priorities for the rest of the day.

It's nice to know that You needed a break in Your busy schedule too. I guess You must have felt like I do sometimes, that You had entirely too many people needing something—and all needing it *now. ASAP!* You had so many people clamoring for Your attention, so many souls to save, heal, cleanse, bless, and feed.

Thanks, Lord, for being with me all the time, not just in these few minutes when I really focus on You. I'm ready now to go back in and face the anxious customers and demanding bosses. I'll try to work diligently as You did and take the time to listen, teach,

and graciously give of myself to those who are in
need.

Prayer

*Dear Jesus, help me follow Your example and take
time away when job pressures seem overwhelming. Give
me rest and peace in You. In Your name. Amen.*

A Death
in the Family

You will grieve, but your grief will turn to
joy. *John 16:20*

A co-worker's husband died yesterday. As the
news wove its way through the grapevine, an eerie
stillness echoed through the bank. People sat at their
desks, silently praying for their fellow employee. We
answered phones and took care of customers, but no
one truly concentrated on the work at hand.

"What can we do? How can we help her through
this tragic loss? What about food?" We tried to come up
with ways to soothe the loss, but it all seemed so inadequate. As a sympathy card went around, each person
took a little extra time to think of the right words to say.
"We're praying and thinking of you. I'm so sorry. We
care." But no one could come up with just the right
words to say what was felt deep in the heart.

We were a little kinder to each other yesterday. We were a little gentler with the elderly man's complaint and a young mother's crying child. No one griped about the work load.

I called my husband in the middle of the day, suddenly grateful to hear his voice. I didn't care anymore that he had forgotten to take out the trash. I paused to say a silent prayer of thanks.

Prayer

Lord, sometimes we don't count our blessings until we share in someone else's tragedy. Please give those dealing with loss or suffering in any way Your peace. Wrap Your loving arms around them and hold them. Thank You for reminding me of Your many blessings and help me not to take them for granted. In Your name. Amen.

Cowardly ... or Courteous?

The tongue of the wise commends knowledge, but the mouth of the fool gushes folly. *Proverbs 15:2*

The woman constantly interrupted the speaker. Long-winded stories detailed how her department handled situations differently. She rudely argued and complained.

A few times the speaker tried to regain control of the meeting. "Let's move on," she graciously said. But the woman kept interrupting.

I wished the speaker would counterattack the outbursts, tell the woman to shut up. But the speaker was too well-mannered for such abrasive behavior. Knowing she had lost control of the meeting, the speaker called an early break and left the room.

I thought the speaker had taken the cowardly way out by avoiding a confrontation with the woman. Then I noticed the speaker had poured the heckler a cup of coffee and asked her to a corner table. In a kind yet firm voice, the speaker told the woman how much she valued her input, but there simply wasn't enough time to get through the material and still listen to her "ideas."

When the meeting resumed, the speaker courteously, but firmly, told the group the same message. She added that she would gladly take any suggestions or comments during the discussion time at the end of the meeting.

The speaker never lost her temper—or her manners. She remained polite and respectful even in the face of rudeness and impertinence.

Prayer

Help me remember, Lord, that You gave me two ears and only one mouth for a good reason. When the urge to speak overcomes the will to listen, let my words be as gracious as those of the speaker. Remind me that politeness can be the loudest and strongest voice of all. And when my mouth takes over, forgive me for the sake of Your Son. In His name. Amen.

I'll Fix the Fax, Got a Hammer?

Be joyful in hope, patient in affliction.
Romans 12:12

Why do I always set off the burglar alarm? Why does my computer forget how to compute and my typewriter forget how to type? In the ongoing battle with machines, I always lose.

They're all against me.

I think the copy machine recognizes my perfume. When it smells me coming, the toner light flashes a warning and the paper runs for cover deep inside a black hole.

The printer refuses to awaken until after I've had my morning coffee. It's in cahoots with the phone line. Incoming calls made before 9 a.m. are automatically routed to me, and outgoing calls go to the woman who scolds, "The number you have dialed ..." I don't trust either one of them.

But the leader of the machine brigade is the fax machine. "Cannot Transmit" camouflages my computer's sneak attack. As I send and resend the fax, my computer busily bytes away at the data it's supposed to be processing. It finishes every last morsel before spitting out an empty disk. And while I'm unjamming the fax paper, my calculator has time to jumble a few numbers.

I've had it! I launch an offensive, firing rubber

bands at the computer, but it eats them too. I attack the copy machine with one of those tiny screwdrivers; it squeals and sputters, but the toner light refuses to retreat. The machines have won again.

What I need is some heavy artillery. Then I'll strike at the heart of the brigade—that dreaded, terrorist fax machine.

Bring me that hammer!

Prayer

Dear Lord, give me patience and peace when things go wrong. Fill me with Your Spirit so that I will rejoice when things go right. Help me see that in all things, You are working good for me. In Jesus' name. Amen.

The 25-Year-Old Boss

Then I was the craftsman at His side.
I was filled with delight day after day.
Proverbs 8:30

I have more experience; he has a college degree.

I drive a dusty station wagon; he drives a shiny sports car.

I have three teenagers; he's still single.

I hoe the garden; he works out at the athletic club.

I go to PTA meetings; he goes to assertiveness training.

I muddle my way through DOS; he creates programs.

I spend the weekend doing laundry; he goes skiing.

I read *Better Homes and Gardens;* he reads the *Wall Street Journal.*

We make a pretty good team.

He admires my experience; I appreciate his youthful energy.

He paid for my computer class; I edited his annual report.

He brings in fresh ideas; I tell him whether they're practical.

He makes the coffee; I bring homemade cookies.

He longs for a family; I can't wait for some time to myself.

Now if I can just convince him to trade cars.

Prayer

Lord, thank You for my boss. Thank You for his energy, his willingness to listen, and his enthusiasm. He makes the job fun. Help us work as a team. Continue to give me a gracious attitude that will brighten our partnership and enable our mutual efforts to bear fruit. And let my words and actions be a witness to Your Son's servitude and saving grace. In His name. Amen.

Get Organized?

There is a time for everything, and a
season for every activity under heaven.
Ecclesiastes 3:1

"Mrs. Roberts, did you forget that your son had a
dental appointment this morning?" The receptionist
sounded irritated. I thought the appointment was
tomorrow.

"You know we'll have to charge you for an office
call," she added.

That was it. I determined to become more organized. I went to the office supply store and bought a
nifty organizer notebook, the kind all the power people pack around. Life is put into neat little sections:
menu, goals, finances, even vitamin intake. I organized
my life, and my family's, into a series of lists.

For about a month.

To haul the dictionary-size book around, I needed a briefcase. The planning system seemed a little too
complicated for me, and the kids didn't mark off a single box on the bedroom cleaning list.

I bought a more condensed purse-size version. Of
course nothing else fit in my purse, so I bought a bigger shoulder bag. Soon my neck went out from haul-
ing the big satchel.

My teenage son informed me about the latest in
technology, the electronic organizer. Being organized
was very expensive! He assured me it was as easy to
operate as the VCR. Wonderful. Then the batteries

gave out and I "lost my memory." Brain dead.

Finally, I found the perfect organizer. It's a small tapestry-covered notebook that was on sale for $5.99. There's a slot in the front for my checkbook and a little pouch for stamps, an emery board, and an extra car key that comes in handy when I lock myself out. The notebook has a monthly appointment calendar with 2"-square boxes for each day. A lined notepad serves as the to-do list (it says nothing about dusting baseboards).

The slot for my driver's license holds a prayer card instead. It has a picture of Jesus carrying a tired lamb in one arm and a staff in the other. His eyes look down lovingly at His precious cargo—me.

Prayer

Lord, thank You for helping me realize that life is not a series of categories sectioned off into lists. Life is a series of surprises. Some are good, like an unexpected date with my husband. Some aren't so good, like a broken syrup bottle on Monday morning. But through all of life's ups and downs, You are there, guiding me to still waters and green pastures. And You even carry me when things get too tough. Thank You for Your constant love and care, Jesus. In Your name. Amen.

The Promotion

I can do everything through Him who
gives me strength. *Philippians 4:7*

I got the job! Thank You, Lord. I'm excited and
exhilarated, like the football player who does a back
flip after scoring the winning touchdown. Yes! *Yes!*

I'm also scared to death. Can I really do the job?
What if I fall flat on my face? There's so much I still
have to learn about the position: new computer programs, laws, regulations, calculations. Can I do it?

And what about my family? Will they be able to
adjust to my longer hours? Will I be too stressed or too
tired to be a caring, effective parent and spouse?

Can I really do it all? I'm a far cry from being
superwoman. I don't have a bionic brain. I'm not
invincible. Yes, I love a challenge, but I also need time
to recharge and reflect.

Lord, with Your strength I've been able to tackle
some pretty difficult times and some tough jobs. With
Your help I've met challenges head-on. Your power is
strong enough to give me the determination to succeed, both at home and at work. Your presence in my
life will get me through the new computer system and
help me juggle my career and family.

Prayer

*Thank You for believing in me, Lord, even when, espe-
cially when, I doubt my abilities. Thank You for giving me
Your Word, the manual I can turn to when I'm stuck or*

have lost myself entirely. I know that with You as my manager, I'll be able to handle whatever comes. Yes! YES! In Jesus' name. Amen!

Coming in Second

A time to tear and a time to mend.
Ecclesiastes 3:7

I got the promotion and she didn't. I know how much she wanted the job, but I wanted it too. And I'm really not sorry I got it. I don't feel like I should apologize for anything. I've worked hard for many years, and I'm proud that I've earned the respect of my supervisors.

When others were patting me on the back, she was in the back room crying. She rained on my parade. I understand her anger and disappointment. She's been here longer and her qualifications are good. She could have done the job.

It's hard to come in second, to lose the race by a couple of feet. The hardest games to lose are those that are lost by only one point.

I may have won the job but I've lost something—a friend. Her icy stares and the cold shoulders from her friends in the department have frozen me out. Yesterday, when I walked into the room and chattering turned to silence, it was obvious who they had been discussing. And now everyone has been invited to her

Tupperware party. Everyone but me.

It hurts, Lord, to know that my gain has caused a friend pain. But what hurts worse is knowing that what I thought was a good friendship was actually weak and shallow.

Prayer

Dear Lord, the next time I come in second, don't let my disappointment rain on someone else's parade. Even if I think the race was unfair, give me the dignity to be a good loser. Help me swallow my pride and offer a congratulatory hand to the winner. And Lord, help me to be a gracious and humble winner. Don't let me hold a grudge against those who curse my victory. In Jesus' name. Amen.

Oh, Nuts!

Whatever your hand finds to do, do it
with all your might. *Ecclesiastes 9:10*

I really blew it this time. How could I make such a stupid mistake? Thankfully someone caught my error before it caused too much damage.

What was I thinking about? My mind definitely wasn't focused on the task at hand. What I thought was a menial, boring job was actually extremely important. My mistake could have cost the company a lot of money. At least my boss was able to laugh about it. "So much for perfection," he chuckled.

Sometimes I think I am perfect, but this mistake sure knocked me down a notch or two. Next time I'll be more careful. I'll double-check my figures and make sure the job is done right—no matter how small or meaningless the project.

It reminds me of a saying I learned in grade school:

Don't worry if your job is small and your
rewards are few; remember that the mighty
oak was once a nut like you.

Prayer

Lord, I guess it's pretty nutty to think that any task can be done haphazardly. It definitely takes more time to explain why something went wrong than to do it right the first time. Help me learn from this mistake. In Jesus' name. Amen.

Bloom Where You Are Planted

Commit to the Lord whatever you do, and your plans will succeed. *Proverbs 16:3*

I feel stuck in this job, Lord. Don't get me wrong, I'm grateful for the work. On the morning news they said 10,000 people applied for only 500 jobs in Chicago. People seem desperate for a job ... any job. Mothers are unable to put food on the table for their children. Fathers are unable to buy clothing for their families.

Yes, I'm thankful for my job, but sometimes I want to be more than someone's employee. I want to work for You. I want to feel more useful. I want to help others. I *need* to share my blessings, but how can I do that as a secretary? What difference can I make by filing and typing?

I trust You to guide me. I trust You to show me how I can make a difference, no matter how small. I trust You to nurture me as I do my work to Your glory. I depend on You to move me to share the Gospel with my co-workers and customers. Help me be a light on a hill.

Prayer

Help me, Lord, to bloom where I'm planted. In Jesus' name. Amen.

Giving Up

Be strong and courageous, and do the work. Do not be afraid or discouraged, for the Lord God, my God, is with you. He will not fail you or forsake you. *1 Chronicles 28:20*

I want to give up. I thought my idea was good; I

expected praise and encouragement. Instead, they squashed my idea like a bug on a sidewalk.

Please, Lord, lift me out of my discouragement. Give me strength to get up and try again. Help me know when to let go and when to keep at it, even if others say it can't be done.

Help me pull my tail out from between my shaky legs and take a hard look at my idea. Help me clear away the anger and see if the critics are right or if there actually is a way to make the idea germinate and flower. Plant in me a new determination. And if I truly believe the idea can be fruitful, give me the strength to go forward. Help me avoid stubborn pride, which can cloud my judgment.

Remind me, Lord, that criticism isn't a personal attack and that rejection of my idea isn't a rejection of me. Keep me from burying my ideas out of fear. Instead, fan the fires of my imagination. Help me know when to hold fast, and when to let go. Don't let me take the easy way out by simply giving up … or giving in.

Just let me give.

Prayer

Father, You turned defeat into victory for Your people time and time again. When the Israelites trembled in fear between the sea and the Egyptians, You parted the waters. When we fell into sin and faced defeat and death at Satan's hands, You sent Jesus to suffer and die in our place. When I stumble here on earth, put the cross before my eyes. Remind me that I already have the greatest victory through my Savior, who still fights by my side. In Jesus' name. Amen.

Who Put the Rose on My Desk?

A gift opens the way for the giver.
Proverbs 18:16

Never easy to get along with, my co-worker's increasingly abrasive manner is causing additional problems. I've also heard rumors that she's having trouble at home. Well, I've tried to be patient, but her cross and surly attitude has been more irritating than usual.

I asked her to help a customer. I got a snippy comeback about being late for lunch. I snapped back. When she came back from lunch, her eyes looked red and swollen. She didn't speak to anyone and left early. I was still too angry to care.

The next morning, a blushing pink rose was lying on my desk. There was no card. I asked around, but no one admitted to the small act of kindness. Then I saw an identical pink rose on the desk of the woman who had made me so angry.

She sheepishly acknowledged she had been the giver.

"It's called a peace rose," she quietly added. "I grew it myself."

Apology accepted.

Prayer

Lord, help me look beyond the actions of others to the

pain or the fear that may be the cause. Help me look for unspoken signals that a helping hand is needed instead of a cross word. Give me an extra measure of Your Holy Spirit so that I may be the one to extend the hand of forgiveness when I'm cross with a fellow employee. Give me a humble heart to accept another's apology and offer forgiveness. In Jesus' name. Amen.

The Takeover

I will fear no evil, for You are with me.
Psalm 23:4

I'm afraid. I hoped it was only a rumor, but today's memo confirmed my fears. The bank is being bought out by a Midwestern conglomerate. The buy out seems so mechanical and impersonal.

And now we wait; we're told it's a numbers game. There's a model to fill, and we'll all fit in a slot—at least they hope we'll all fit. The new Human Resources department will let us know.

Our futures are on the line, or should I say, on the model. Our fates lie in the hands of nameless and faceless people in Minneapolis. But do those people know that Kathy is a single parent, the sole means of support for her two children? Do they realize that Pat's husband has terminal cancer? Do they understand how much I love my job?

Does big business realize we're human? That we

aren't plastic pieces on a chessboard? That some of us have house payments and can't make it without health insurance? Has top management forgotten the fear of losing not only a job but a way of life? Of losing an extended family, people with whom we spend a third of our life?

Prayer

Please, Jesus, help me trust You during this difficult time. Please help "Human" Resources remember that we are indeed human. In Your name. Amen.

Upper Management

The man who plants and the man who waters have one purpose. *1 Corinthians 3:8*

We just got another memo stressing teamwork. The company has a common goal, the memo notes, we all need to work together as a team.

If we're a team, why do I feel like we're playing on completely different fields sometimes? The line, however fine, has been drawn. It is them—upper management—and us. If they are *upper*, then what are we, *lower?* Lower what?

How did You do it, Lord? How did You manage Your disciples? You were clearly in charge, but I can't imagine that You dined on quail while Your disciples dined on bread. You listened to their questions, suggested solutions, challenged them to state what they believed. You walked beside them, not in front. You guided them just as You guide me.

Yes, it's true that without managers there would be chaos. Someone needs to determine the goals, motivate, encourage, and even set the rules. And someone has to referee the inevitable squabbles. But it's hard to hear management if they're in the penthouse dining on steak while the employees are in the basement eating peanut butter.

Prayer

Lord, You brought very different individuals together and formed them into a team to spread the news of Your death and resurrection. You taught Your disciples to work together. Through my Baptism, You made me a member of Your team too. Help me witness this team spirit in my professional life as well as in my spiritual life. Help upper management and employees find a middle ground to accomplish the goals of our company. Help us work as a team because without teamwork, both sides lose. In Jesus' name. Amen.

A Pain in the Neck

A patient man has great understanding,
but a quick-tempered man displays folly.
Proverbs 14:29

Where is my compassion, Lord? The customer is such a ... well, honestly, she's a pain in the neck.

This woman demands an immense amount of my time with her endless questions and constant complaints. Nothing ever suits her. It seems the harder I try to accommodate her absurd needs, the more she demands.

I know she's lonely, Lord. She alienates her family with her overbearing attitude. Frankly, I've run out of patience too. She's pushed me to the limit one too many times.

What do I do now? I try to imagine how You would handle her latest complaint. What would You say to her, Lord?

I just realized, You never get tired of my unending questions. And despite all my complaints, You still give me everything I need in this life. You even gave me my faith in Jesus, my Savior. You're always there to lead the way.

Prayer

Lord, help me follow Your lead. Give me patience to respectfully listen to Your guidance and respond in love. When people demand more than I can possibly give, show me how to be firm yet kind. Help me, through my own atti-

tude, to gently lead others into Your light by patiently listening to their demands, just as You listen to mine. In Jesus' name. Amen.

A Cup of Insani ... tea

A cheerful heart is good medicine. *Proverbs 17:22*

If one more person puts something on my desk, I'll go crazy. If one more customer gives me some lame excuse about overdrawing a checking account, I'll let loose a loud, primal scream of frustration. And if that phone rings one more time with someone complaining about our pig ad on television, I'll yank the phone out of the wall.

That's it! I've had it. I'm out of here. I'm sick of this job—the customers, the paperwork, the broken copy machine, my grouchy boss. I need a break.

The coffee reminds me of the oil in my car—cold and gummy. Maybe I'll just have a cup of tea. Great, all that's left is the lemon herb flavor. It tastes like moldy weeds, but at least it's hot.

Did that woman really think I would believe that her dog ate her teller machine card? I have to admit, the story is well worth the $10 charge for the card. I guess I'll rebate it after all.

Prayer

Lord, thank You for this silly, heartwarming cup of insani ... tea. Thanks for helping me laugh at this stressful, overworked, and underpaid job. Well, at least it's never boring. As I face whatever else this crazy job may bring, help me get through the rest of my day with

a dash of humili ... tea;
a sprig of sereni ... tea;
a healthy dose of tranquili ... tea;
and just a little bit of gaie ... tea.

A cheerful heart really is the best medicine. I'm feeling much better now. Thanks, Lord. Amen.

SECTION 2

WHO LOST THE INSTRUCTION BOOK?

The Resumé

What does man gain from all his labor
at which he toils under the sun?
Ecclesiastes 1:3

What do I put on this resumé? Where, on the one-page synopsis of my life, do I place all I have learned and accomplished?

Can balancing a checkbook, budgeting grocery money, or saving a few dollars a month for college be noted as accounting experience?

Can clapping over a toddler's first steps, helping a child with a term paper, or handing over the car keys to a 16-year-old Mario Andretti be deemed teaching ability?

Can feeding a family of six on one pound of hamburger be classified as budget management skills?

Can cleaning gravel from skinned knees and administering hot pink medicine to stomach flu victims be interpreted as nursing skills?

Can clean clothes, warm hugs, and full tummies demonstrate excellent customer relations?

Can the ability to put up with a house full of relatives, turn the other cheek to a sarcastic teenager, or referee sibling rivalry be construed as public relations skills?

Can conducting musical chairs at a birthday

party or making sure children do their chores be listed as supervisory experience?

Can 20 years of learning to be a good parent, wife, housekeeper, seamstress, chef, counselor, mechanic, gardener, lawyer, and nurse qualify me for a degree in domestic engineering?

Does "The School of Hard Knocks" qualify as a reputable educational institution?

Under reason for leaving present job do I write "Desires to enter a new field where salary is commensurate with responsibilities and there are better opportunities for advancement"? Maybe I'll just put "Seeks to improve status."

And what about references? Is it acceptable to put school teachers, Little League coaches, or a mother-in-law who actually likes me? Maybe it would be wise to add "Please do not contact current employer until after interview."

Prayer

Lord, staying home and raising small children doesn't look very impressive on a resumé. But it was such an important job and certainly the hardest thing I've ever done. Now that I'm out looking for a "real" job, lead me to an employer who will respect me and give my position as "mom" the credibility it deserves. Give me strength for the search and trust in Your plan for my life. In Jesus' name. Amen.

Mom's Vacation

Rest in the shadow of the Almighty.
Psalm 91:1

I take a bubble bath in the hotel bathroom and no one knocks at the door.

I have the king-size bed all to myself and no one steals the covers.

Shopping bags cover the aqua chair and no little hands prowl through the contents.

I turn on the television and no one punches the remote control.

The heater hums in the corner and no one complains that it's too hot.

I put my tea from room service on the nightstand and no one has spilled a drop.

It's a quiet, peaceful room and no one's socks are on the floor but mine.

So why can't I go to sleep?

I call the familiar number and tell the little voice on the other end to sleep tight.

The big voice says that all is fine.

I surf the channels with the remote control.

I lay the pillow long ways beside me and turn the heater down.

I reach for the cup of tea and spill some of the amber liquid on the soft white sheets.

Much better.

What a great vacation!

Lord, thank You for rest and relaxation. Amen.

His First Words

He gathers the lambs in His arms and carries them close to His heart; He gently
leads those that have young. *Isaiah 40:11*

My son said his first word today, Lord. It wasn't
Dada or *Mama*. It sounds just like his baby-sitter's
name, Nan. She was so proud, telling me all about it
when I picked him up after work. He gave her a hug
and tightly held onto her when I tried to take him.

Sometimes I think my child likes the sitter more
than he likes me. Is that why I'm angry with her? Nan
is all I could ask for in a baby-sitter: kind, caring,
patient, and loving. She disciplines gently and never
yells. She sings silly songs and plays follow the leader.

I didn't witness my son's first steps. Nan did. I
didn't hear his first words. Nan did. But I did hear his
second word, a resounding *no!* when Nan told him it
was time to go home. And with all the motherly support she could give me, Nan firmly stated it was natural for him to want to stay and play with his other
little friends. But I understood that he really wanted
to be with her.

I'm actually jealous!

How I envy her, Lord. She doesn't have to dress

up for work, and she can be home with her own children while she helps other parents.

But strangely enough, the other day Nan said she envies me. She misses getting dressed up and talking to adults. She misses going to lunch with friends, and she sometimes feels like a prisoner in her own home. The kids tie her down. Even a haircut becomes a major outing.

Lord, I'm sorry I was angry with Nan. I'm sorry I wasn't there to hear my son's first word, but I'm thankful that Nan was there to listen.

She has a thankless job. No incentive bonus, no fringe benefits except witnessing the accomplishments of childhood. Help me remember how hard it is to stay home with children, day after day ... to nurture and love, discipline and cuddle. Wiping away drool and changing diapers may not be a high-powered, executive position, but it's one of the most important and most honorable jobs in the world.

Prayer

Thank You, Lord, for baby-sitters who make working women's jobs a little easier. Help me not to envy their position. Help me respect and admire their devotion to my children. Enable me to reward and praise them for the important job they do. Give them strength and a tender spirit as they shepherd Your little lambs. In Jesus' name. Amen.

Day Care? But I Care

[Jesus] took the children in His arms, put
His hands on them and blessed them.
Mark 10:16

The first woman's house was clean. Too clean.

The next woman's house was a little too dirty.

The day care center was nice. The kids seemed to
have fun. Teachers taught the children the ABCs and
helped them make God's eyes from craft sticks and
yarn. But there were so many children. And so few
people to attend to the little ones' needs.

Maybe going back to work was the wrong decision. My 3-year-old was ready for playmates, but what
if the children at the center weren't the right ones?
Would they share? Did their parents teach them the
same values I was teaching my son? One day, he got
sick at the day care center. He woke from his nap, crying and feverish. But I wasn't there to comfort him.
Did anyone?

Now he's 16 years old. He has a part-time job. He
can run the washing machine. He manages his own
savings account. He's becoming a strong, independent
young man. He picks me up for lunch and tells me
how his day is going. I tell him about mine.

He survived the day care center.

So did I.

Prayer

Lord, thank You for people who care for children.

Encourage and empower them to share Your love with the little ones in their care. In Jesus' name. Amen.

The Whispering Vaporizer

I was sick and you looked after Me.
Matthew 25:36

He comes into the bedroom at 2 a.m., gasping for air. He's terrified. So am I.

Croup. How many times have I sat in this steamy bathroom in the middle of the night, holding one of my children, stroking his hair, softly singing away our fears?

What blessed relief when my child begins to relax, when the short gasping breaths melt into longer sighs. What comforting exhaustion when my child and I finally curl up together in bed.

Then, listening to the lullaby of the whispering vaporizer, we drift into slumber.

Prayer

Lord, with a sleepy sigh, I thank You. Not just for watching over my child but for watching over me. For easing his cough. For easing my worry. Thank You for Your healing hand. Now we both can rest. In Your name. Amen.

The Perfect Present

May those who love you be secure. May there
be peace within your walls. *Psalm 122:6–7*

My son asked me at breakfast what I wanted for
my birthday. I quickly answered, "One day of peace
and quiet!"

With three teenagers and a 5-year-old, peace and
quiet is only available from midnight to 6 a.m. And
even then the dog barks at the moon and the grandfather clock chimes on the hour.

I envisioned the perfect present as I put away the
cereal, ironed a skirt, paid a couple of bills, and
dressed for work:

A day off of work. No laundry. No phone
constantly ringing. No dishes, clean or dirty.
No early morning arguments. No spilled
milk. And no worrying over grades, fax
machines, friends, peer pressure, curfews …

But my birthday fell on Thursday, so I pulled on
my power suit and dashed out the door. I put out fires,
not on a birthday cake but at the job. I answered
phones, settled feuds, and sent faxes.

I came home too tired to go out to dinner, so we
ordered pizza. I blew out 10 candles on the store-bought
cake my husband picked up on his way home from
work. Ten was all the kids could find in the junk drawer.

All in all, it wasn't much of a celebration. I felt
one year older and none the wiser. But I did take an

extra long bubble bath and ignored the laundry room. I went to bed early and picked up my Bible. Psalms seemed appropriate; I needed some comfort.

"May those who love you be secure. May there be peace within your walls."

Ah, peace. That's what I had really wanted. Instead, I received stress wrapped up with a big red bow. And a new blouse to go under my power suit.

I read the verse again. "May those who love you be secure ..."

Funny. I read it one more time. "May those who love you ..."

I could have sworn that the first time I read the verse it said, "May those *you* love ..."

Maybe that's what I thought it *should* have said. In trying to be the responsible parent, loving wife, and efficient employee, I was so wrapped up in doing all the loving, worrying, and fretting that I had forgotten to unwrap the most important gift of all—their love for me.

The perfect present of love doesn't always come in pretty paper with a shiny bow. It's often hidden in a hug and buried under packing material that keeps the precious gift from getting cracked.

No, I never got the peace and quiet I asked for on my birthday list.

I got something better.

Prayer

Thank You, Father, for another year. And thank You

for this rowdy, noisy bunch that love me as much as I love them. Thank You for Your presence in our lives. You have given us the perfect example of love in Your greatest gift—Jesus. Help us treasure each other, our faith, and our ability to share Your love with each other. In Jesus' name. Amen.

The Neglected Son

Do not withhold good ... when it is in
your power to act. *Proverbs 3:27*

My son's second-grade teacher just called. He's having a little trouble in school. Nothing serious, she reassures me. If it's not serious, then why is she calling?

He seems tired, she reports. And he was rough-housing with another boy in the coatroom. The behavior isn't typical for him, she says, and adds that maybe it's just spring fever. Could I talk to him?

As my son hops off the bus, I'm home to greet him, thankfully. Last week I was out of town for four days at a seminar. I notice he needs a haircut, something that should have been done two weeks ago. His fingernails need trimming too. There's enough dirt under them to plant a pumpkin seed.

We haven't enjoyed an after-school walk or read a bedtime story together for more than a month. His pants look too short, and his favorite shirt is missing a button. His jacket is dirty as well. I'm such a terrible mother, God. I'm so sorry that I've neglected him.

I turn off the computer and set aside my nearly completed work as he walks in the house. If I just had a couple more hours … I shove several half-finished ideas into the back of my brain, hoping I will find them when I turn the mind machine back on.

I welcome him with a hug and a kiss and pack him into the car. I drop my son off at the barbershop and run to the store to pick up the milk I should have bought yesterday. My son is waiting when I return. He looks shiny and clean, except for the dirt under his nails.

On the way home, I tell him that his teacher called. "Sorry, Mamma." He gives me a sad look that reminds me of a puppy that's been scolded for chewing a favorite shoe.

"I'm sorry too. I missed your open house last week, didn't I?"

"Uh-huh."

After dinner I herd him into the bathtub. I clip his fingernails, and he holds up his toes. "These too?" he grins. We snuggle together under a comforter on the couch, and he shows me a story he's been writing about a boy named Miguel who's searching for a lost sheep. He asks me how to spell a few words, even though I think he already knows them.

I tell him it's time for bed.

"Just a little longer, please? I really want to finish this," he pleads. I understand all too well. He writes THE END in big block letters, and I tuck him into bed. He smells clean and his hair looks neat. I would love to crawl in beside him and hold him until he falls asleep, but his laundry hamper is overflowing. I grab a pile of little blue jeans. I take his jacket off the hook and pull out the treasures in the pockets: rocks, a whistle, a broken crayon, a crumbled cookie. I tell him I'll be right back and head to the laundry room.

A few minutes later, after picking his cars up off the living-room floor, I look in on my son. But he's sound asleep. His hair is already mussed, and I comb it with my fingers and whisper, "I love you."

He smiles. I think he heard me.

Prayer

Lord, forgive me. I don't mean to neglect my son. Help me order my priorities and give me energy to serve my family as well as to do my job. And thank You. Thank You for the teacher who took time from her own busy day to call me, to give me a kindly jolt. It's a comfort to know he has a teacher who cares. And I care too. Even when I forget to show it. It's good to know that when I'm not the perfect parent, You forgive me. You are the perfect Father. And through the faith in Jesus that You gave me, I have become Your child. Thanks in my Savior's name. Amen.

Fried Mice

Wise men store up knowledge.
Proverbs 10:14

Oh, no. Not again. My son needs a project for the

science fair. He wants to grow mold. I wonder if he has looked in the back of the refrigerator lately.

I remember when my daughter first spoke those words that give parents nightmares, "science fair project." She excitedly declared that for her experiment she was going to see how light helps things grow.

"Good idea, dear," I calmly encouraged.

"All I need are some Christmas lights, some wooden boxes, and a few mice."

"Mice!"

"Sure, what did you think I was going to use?"

"Pumpkin seeds or beans."

My little scientist reassured me she would feed them and clean their cages every day. I let out a resounding, "No! No mice!"

But it was for science. Didn't I want her to do well in school? She acted like she was going after the Nobel prize and made me feel like I was blocking the cure for cancer. The things we parents do for our children. And it's usually the parents who really get the education.

We went to the pet store and bought five white mice, mouse food, and cedar chips to line the wooden boxes. We hauled a box out of the garage and pulled out the Christmas lights. She weighed each mouse with my diet scales and wrote the information on poster board. One mouse would live in total darkness, one in red light, one in blue, one in green, and one in natural light. She tucked the mice into their new homes and threatened the cat who was lurking by the door.

Someone should have warned the little scientist about one very important fact. Christmas lights give off an immense amount of heat. When she removed the lid the next day, the mouse in the red-light box had died of heat exposure. The boxes with blue and green lights housed mice that were barely alive.

My daughter's project wasn't a total loss. After one month of living in darkness, one of the surviving mice had grown fat and lazy. The mouse that lived in natural light became bored in his little cage and ran around in circles. Just before the project was due, he ate a hole through the wooden box and disappeared to parts unknown. (Actually, I think the cat has a good idea where it went.) Even with only one very fat, lazy mouse left, the project earned my daughter a B+. I guess her science teacher has kids too.

And now my son wants to grow mold? I convinced him to do his report on batteries. Don't stop learning, but don't make the same mistake twice.

Prayer

Lord, thank You for such intelligent children. You have given them creativity and the desire to learn. Help me appreciate this and not dampen their inquisitive nature—even when it conflicts with my schedule or my tolerance of small furry animals. Help me build on past experiences to meet the challenges that arise every day. Give me an extra measure of patience and strengthen my trust in You for the guidance to be a supportive parent. In Jesus' name. Amen.

The Child in Me

Jesus said, "Let the little children come to Me, and do not hinder them, for the kingdom of heaven belongs to such as these."
Matthew 19:14

There's a secret I don't let anyone see. Deep inside this tough-minded working woman, mother of four, and grandmother of two, hides a little girl. She peeks out from time to time, wondering if it's safe to come out and play. She's a little nymph in pigtails who loves to romp through green fields and swing high in the treetops.

When this little girl emerges, gone is the facade of the sophisticated career woman. Gone is the serious-minded, responsible maturity that has developed from being "grown-up."

Sometimes the little girl is sad. When someone says something mean or cruel to the "grown-up," the little child longs for warm arms to cuddle her and soft hands to wipe away the tears.

Sometimes the child is full of joy and silliness. She does goofy things like trying to walk down the sidewalk without stepping on a crack. And when she feels like doing a cartwheel, the grown-up reminds her to see first if anyone is watching. Often she does it anyway; she's kind of a show-off.

Sometimes the child is a little bit naughty. She's been known to hide her brussels sprouts under a napkin at an elite dinner party. And just last week she complained of a stomachache when she didn't want to go to the board meeting. She can be rebellious, and she whines to go home when she's tired. Most of the time though, the little girl is a good kid.

Sometimes the child is wistful as she ponders the many questions of life: how geese always find their way back home, how a fuzzy caterpillar transforms into a beautiful butterfly, how a tiny foal emerges from its mother and instantly stands to nurse. There are questions that even her bright, childish imagination can't answer: Where is heaven? Do angels wear clothes? If God loves her friend, why did He let her get hurt?

It's strange, but the more "mature" the grown-up me gets, the more the little girl emerges. The gate that used to be locked tight swings open more frequently, allowing her to come out and play. Maybe with age and the raging storms of life, those old fences—like that high-minded fence of "What would people say?"—have started breaking down.

The other day the child hopped out as the grown-up watched my grandson experience a rainstorm. The two children held out their hands and tried to catch the crystal drops that fell from the sky. They were fascinated by the feel, the smell, and the sound of the rain falling. They sloshed through puddles in the cooling summer shower, soaking in the splendor of the cleansing rain.

I hope the little girl can come out and play tomorrow. She's so much fun!

Prayer

Father, You have made me Your child in the waters of

Baptism. Help me never to lose the ability to look at Your creation with the wide eyes of a child. Even in my "mature" years, give me a joyful spirit, one that willingly witnesses to Your presence in my life. In Jesus' name. Amen.

Why Can't My Child Read?

I am the Lord your God, who teaches you
what is best for you, who directs you in
the way you should go. *Isaiah 48:17*

Lord, what's wrong? Last night we studied his spelling words for more than an hour, and tonight they're a jumble of letters. Other children his age took to reading like kites in a strong wind. He rises and falls like a kite without a tail.

He needs help, but I don't know how to give it to him. I talked to his teacher, and she said that kids learn at their own pace. He just needs to try a little harder, concentrate. But Lord, I know how hard he tries. I see the disappointment and frustration on his young face when his papers are returned with a sad face because they're too sloppy.

I try to read to him, but he can't sit still for five minutes. He'd rather be taking his bike apart—and then putting it back together. He has the fastest bike on the block, but he can't put together a simple sentence.

Now they want to hold him back a year to repeat third grade. Is it the right thing to do? Or will it further shatter his already delicate ego?

Prayer

Lord, help me make the right decision. Educate me as a parent. Help me know and do the right thing for my child. Help me trust Your promise to work in all things for good. In Jesus' name. Amen.

Please Pass the Meat Loaf

She provides food for her family.
Proverbs 31:15

I can't remember the last time my family sat down together for an old-fashioned family dinner—meat loaf, mashed potatoes, vegetables, salad, and dessert. Staples such as flour and sugar have been replaced by Hamburger Helper and frozen pizza. But when everyone's going in different directions, it's difficult to plan a real family meal. Work, bowling, and basketball practice take priority over dinner together.

As a parent, I tried to shield my children from crime and peer pressure by taking them to all the right places. Sports, church, music, and academics have reassured my parental ego that I'm providing my children with the nurture that will help them grow strong and healthy.

But have I tried too hard? Is my concept of success passing the adult disease of stress onto my kids? Are Little League victories more important than friendly, backyard family games? Do we play catch for fun anymore or is it only to improve the pitching arm? In this race to get ahead, are we actually going nowhere fast?

Lord, this fast-food, take-out, throw-away lifestyle of conveniences and quick fixes is starving my family. Help me slow down and ease up. My children hunger for the attention of a solid family. Help me reevaluate my goals and my family's goals. Let me set the table with Your bounty as the children say grace. Let us come together around the table with You at the head.

Prayer

Come, Lord Jesus, and be our guest. Give us the precious food of Your Word to strengthen us for all the activities in our lives. Bind us together in Your love so that no matter what stresses come at us, we can rest safe in Your arms. Bless us with the gifts of food, fellowship, and faith that only You can give. In Your name. Amen.

Prejudice

*Here there is no Greek or Jew, circumcised
or uncircumcised, barbarian, Scythian,
slave or free, but Christ is all, and is in all.*
Colossians 3:11

I used to think of myself as a free thinker. I would
dare anyone to call me prejudiced … until my daughter dated a Mexican boy. He wreaked havoc in our
household. He convinced her to run away with him. I
quickly began to view all Mexicans through the lenses I used to see him. My feelings were clouded by one
bad incident.

I told a Mexican joke to a friend. Later I heard my
6-year-old son repeating it to a playmate. Without
thinking, I had passed down my prejudice to a future
generation.

Racism happens without warning. One bad experience alters our perception, and we paint all members
of a group with the same brush. Our sinful nature
takes over and we become prejudiced against the
beautiful differences God created in all of us.

That Sunday in church, our bulletin cover pictured children from all around the world holding
hands, encircling the globe. I realized that children
aren't prejudiced by nature—they learn it from their
parents and other adults they meet. Our future is our
children. Isn't it time we taught them the value of
God's creation? Isn't it time we taught them to appreciate our differences as strengths? Isn't it time we

taught them to build each other up instead of to tear each other down? Jesus came to save the *whole* world—not just a particular group.

I asked my son if he understood the picture. He said he did. And with childish honesty, he added that the Asian boy in the picture reminded him of his friend at school. And didn't that African girl look like his friend Keisha who lived next door?

Lord, cleanse me of my prejudice. All flowers are not daisies. All animals are not giraffes. All humans do not have red hair. Therein lies the beauty of Your creation.

Prayer

Lord, sin manifests itself in so many ways. Perhaps the most hurtful way is through prejudice. Even when Your Son walked this earth, groups were discriminated against. Just look at the story of the Good Samaritan. Lord, help me overcome my personal prejudices. Help me pass on to my children a spirit of love and respect for those who are "different"—whether through ability, interests, color of skin, or beliefs. Thank You for forgiving me for the times my prejudices come to the surface. Thank You for the free gift of salvation that unites everyone in Christ. In His name. Amen.

Weekend Warriors

Ascribe to the Lord the glory due His
name; worship the Lord in the splendor of
His holiness. *Psalm 29:2*

Underneath the facade of a responsible, power-suited professional, you'll find an adventurous spirit, someone who can act like Sacajawea, the Shoshone woman who traveled with Lewis and Clark on their expedition to the Pacific Northwest. On Friday nights, my tribe of weekend warriors becomes wandering adventurers, yearning to explore the mountain heights.

No luxuries for these nomads. No bubble baths or electric blankets to warm soggy toes. No easy-to-clean pans; real adventurers use cast-iron skillets. We valiantly weather awesome thunderstorms in a flimsy nylon tent that took several hours to set up. We overcome the adversity of wet firewood, tame wild chipmunks with sunflower seeds, and creep up on a family of beavers.

On Sunday mornings, our cathedral is a glen nestled in a serene aspen grove. Wildflowers grace the altar of freshly washed pines. Trumpets of thunder boom in the background. God is so near, it seems we can almost touch Him. His voice seems to whisper in the breeze.

As we offer our praise and our thanks, all the troublesome worries of working life evaporate. Here, in God's creation, His awesome power is too apparent.

The psalmist's question, "What is man that You are mindful of him?" (8:4) comes to mind. We seem so insignificant here in the mountains. But You, Lord, heard our cries for mercy, and You sent Your Son to be our Savior. You answer all our prayers and provide all we need to live. You truly are an awesome and powerful God.

Prayer

Heavenly Father, we thank You for the majesty of the mountains and for clear lakes so close to the sky they mirror the clouds. Thank You for the owls and the coyotes, for the fish and the deer. Thanks for our senses that allow us to enjoy the world You have given us. Thanks for Jesus, our Savior, whose death and resurrection will bring us into the awesome presence of Your majesty for eternity. In His name. Amen.

The Runaway

Love is patient. *1 Corinthians 13:4*

My hands gripped the steering wheel as the station wagon careened past the lush green lawns of the neighborhood. The fender came dangerously close to a curbside garbage can. I groaned, remembering it was trash day. Mine was still in a heap in the garage. So what. It didn't matter.

I was running away!

I was sick of nagging my kids to clean their rooms and turn down the stereo. I'd had it with melting Popsicles and disputes over who got the biggest piece of cake. I was tired of telling the kids not to lean back in their chairs and to quit bickering. And I was sick of the thankless job of being a mom.

I quit!

The car swerved onto the highway and headed south. I sang loudly to a Beatles tune on the oldies station; salt and pepper hair flew in the wind. I tapped my wedding ring on the side mirror and my bare feet danced on the floorboard.

A fast-food joint waved me in, and I ordered a double cheeseburger and onion rings. I was sick of motherly food too. As I reached in my billfold to pay the carhop, a prayer card fluttered into my lap.

"Love is patient, love is kind," the card read. So what!

But the message played in my mind like a stuck record. What did the apostle Paul know, anyway? He never had four bored kids in the middle of summer vacation. Kids on the phone, teenage heartbreaks, building blocks in the hallway.

"Love is patient ..."

And my husband, too wrapped up in TV sports shows to notice the overflowing trash cans.

"Love is kind ..."

I slurped down the last of the chocolate-banana shake and glanced at my watch. Only a half-hour left to be a runaway! My son's game was at 5:30. I needed to get a move on.

I combed my hair and put on my shoes. I wiped

the sweat from my forehead with a used tissue. As I pulled money out to tip the carhop, four faces smiled from a faded picture in my wallet: one with $2,000 teeth, one still in braces, one missing a tooth, and one still drooling.

"Thank You, God," I whispered aloud, "for these children You have placed in my care. Please, give me patience."

I slowly drove home. Someone had put out the garbage. "Love is …"

"Great, you're home. Have you seen my mitt?"

"It's on the coffee table, right where you left it."

And the melody played on.

Prayer

Thank You, God, for love. Amen.

The Crazies among Us

I will be a Father to you, and you will be My sons and daughters, says the Lord Almighty. *2 Corinthians 6:18*

There are so many crazy people walking among us. Every night the news reports yet another child missing. Every morning, milk cartons greet us with the innocent faces of the lost. Rapists and child molesters are released into our neighborhoods and we have no way of knowing it. The law protects their rights while my children walk home from school unguarded.

I fear for my children, Lord.

I warn them of strangers while the Sunday school lesson teaches of the Good Samaritan. I want them to be helpful, but I also want them to be safe. Is it possible to be both in this age of violence?

I wonder.

I want to protect them from the crazies among us, but to do that, I'd have to clip their wings, the wings they'll need to fly when they're truly on their own. I have to let them go, even though evil may lurk in the shadows. But it's so hard, so scary. I want to hold my innocent ones beside me with a secure leash. I want to guard and protect them.

But they aren't puppies. They're people. I can't chain them inside my enclosure of fear. I must protect their right to a childhood while I protect them from the crazies among us. Somehow I must teach them about showing love and kindness to others, while keeping them out of danger.

Prayer

Dearest Father, help me trust You to protect and watch over my family. Not only are they my children, they are Yours. I know You can protect and guide them, even when I can't. I know You can enable them to grow into caring and trusting adults. Give me the ability to protect them from evil without sacrificing their childhood. In Jesus' name. Amen.

Self-Esteem

Train a child in the way he should go, and
when he is old he will not turn from it.
Proverbs 22:6

The other day my third grader came home with a
handout from the school psychologist entitled
"Developing Your Child's Self-Esteem."

I thumbed through the pages. It gave the following "active parenting" suggestions:

1. Develop positive reinforcement. *Huh?*

2. Encourage independent interaction. *Say what?*

3. Classify "time out" criteria. *Oh, sure.*

I didn't understand any of it. I guess that makes
me a dysfunctional parent. Oh, well, I will blame that
on my dysfunctional childhood. That seems to be
what everyone else is doing nowadays.

My mother was a single parent. I came home to
an empty house—today I would be a latchkey child. I
was expected to do chores and haul in coal for the
stoker. Maybe that was the independent thinking
part. I was grounded for not coming straight home
after school. That was most definitely the "time out"
thing.

And once, at Sunday school, I colored a terrific
picture of Moses and used the funny-smelling white
paste to glue cotton balls on for his beard. Mom was
so proud that she kept it on the refrigerator for more

than a month. Well, so much for blaming my mother or my broken, "dysfunctional" home.

I don't recall any of my classmates having an Ozzie-and-Harriet home. As a matter of fact, we all complained that our parents were unfair dictators out to ruin our lives.

Mom, I didn't thank you then, but I am thanking you now. You were a great parent. You taught me the value of hard work. You taught me to be independent and self-reliant. And I knew you would always be there when I needed a shoulder to cry on or a hand to guide me.

Prayer

Lord, thank You for my parents. I guess good parenting skills go way back. Each generation calls them something different, but they're really the same. Good parents rely on You for guidance. They teach Your rules to their children. Good parents follow Your example of loving interaction and a forgiving attitude. For Jesus' sake, forgive me for the times I fail as a parent. In my Savior's name. Amen.

The Get-Well Card

My grace is sufficient for you, for My power is made perfect in weakness.
2 Corinthians 12:9

Dear Mom,

I hope you will get better today. Do you think you will get better today? I think you will because I love you. Love, your son Todd

Lord, thank You for these days when I'm not expected to be strong. Thank You for this family who wills me to get better with simple and childlike faith. Sometimes it's nice to be weak. Let me give my body time to rest and heal.

When the days come that I'm not quite as strong anymore, don't let me become a burden to my children. Let me plan now for those times when I'll need assistance. Give me the wisdom to tuck away a little bit of each paycheck for my golden years.

Let the love I have for my family be strong enough to keep me healthy and hearty, if not in body, at least in mind. Remind me to save up memories for when I'm old and the children have gone on with their own lives. Make my life full so there will be much to do even without a career.

Prayer

Thank You, healing Father, for the days that I'm weak. Scripture says, "When I am weak, then I am strong." It's comforting to know the power of Your love, and my family's love, is there to help me up when I'm a little shaky and tired. Yes, it's nice to be needed, but once in a while, it's also nice to be in need. For then, I truly feel Your power rest on me. In Jesus' name. Amen.

Privacy

[Jesus said,] "Come with Me by yourselves to a quiet place and get some rest." *Mark 6:31*

All I wanted was a little time to myself—a few precious minutes to relax after the hectic day I'd had at "my real job."

I tried to catch a few minutes by locking the bathroom door, but my daughter needed the blow dryer. I tried to go for a walk, but my youngest son wanted to tag along. I curled up with a magazine on the bed, but my husband wanted to know where I put the Crescent wrench.

I thought I might get a few moments of privacy by asking for help with the dishes. Usually the kids disappear when there's work to do. But even that didn't work this time. My other son asked, since I was in the kitchen, if I would mind bringing him a bowl of ice cream? He needed it for energy to finish his homework. (His favorite excuse.)

I decided to try a different approach, sort of reverse psychology. Instead of asking for privacy, I asked for company.

"Let's all go weed the garden," I cheerfully chirped.

Total silence.

Aha! This is it, I mused, as I grabbed a trowel and headed out the back door. The sweet silence didn't last for long.

"Whatcha doin?" my littlest one asked.

"Weeding the garden. It's really hard work," I said, trying to discourage him. But he wasn't put off. Soon he was digging up worms, and I was off in the garage trying to find a container for his new friends.

Prayer

Lord, is there any quiet place on this planet that a working mother can go to for a little privacy? Help me find peace and quiet and rest in You. In Jesus' name. Amen.

Angel Kisses

Children's children are a crown to the aged, and parents are the pride of their children. *Proverbs 17:6*

My daughter was at that ugly-duckling stage: knobby knees, gangly arms, braces, and the dreaded freckles.

"I'm so ugly, Mom," she cried in self-pity.

I told her she was beautiful. She didn't believe it for a minute.

Then Grandpa came to visit. "How's my beautiful girl?" he asked, giving her one of his famous bear hugs.

"I'm not beautiful at all," she pouted, rambling off her every fault. "The boys tease me because I'm so clumsy. They call me tinsel teeth and say my freckles look like a dot-to-dot book."

"Now just a minute here," he replied. "There's nothing in this world more pretty than a knobby-kneed colt running through a pasture, and some day those teeth will be as straight as the ivory on a piano." He grinned.

"And those freckles, those are nothing more than angel kisses. And judging from that little nose, you must be a pretty wonderful kid to be blessed with so many!"

Prayer

As I watch my daughter walk confidently down the aisle in her sequined dress, I thank You, Lord, for angel kisses and for the wise grandfather who convinced the ugly duckling that someday she would indeed be a swan. In Jesus' name. Amen.

The Miracle

Everyone was amazed and gave praise to God. They were filled with awe and said, "We have seen remarkable things today."
Luke 5:26

Today I witnessed a miracle. A new life came into this world, and I heard the first breath, the first cry. It was beautiful. A blessed, awesome miracle.

The tiny newcomer instantly recognized his mother's voice and searched through swollen eyes for the person talking to him. He sensed something familiar in this new world of bright lights and scary sounds. And he smiled.

The new baby is a unique gift from God. It's truly amazing that of the billions of people who enter this life on earth, each one is special. Each has a unique look and personality. But each tiny person carries a little bit of a living tribute to those who went before him, a legacy of a previous generation. The love that began 21 years ago with a man and a woman now lives on.

It's astounding. This wonderful, tiny miracle is my grandchild … the birth of a new beginning.

As I write baby Daniel's name in my Bible, I notice that there are five names in the birth section—those of my four children and now his.

There's only one name in the death section—Daniel's grandfather. The man who cried with joy when he held his daughter, now Daniel's mother, for the first time.

Even in my joy, I weep that he isn't here to witness this miracle, to hold this infant as he once held his own tiny wonder. But just as Daniel has my daughter's button nose, this child has his grandfather's hands. And that comforts me somehow.

Prayer

Thank You, God, for letting me witness Your gift of life. Help me love and treasure this tiny person in the same way You love us. And thank You that every day, even in something as small as a baby's hand, there's a miracle to be treasured. In Jesus' name. Amen.

Mother's Day

Her children arise and call her blessed.
Proverbs 31:28

I woke to a cup of coffee, a big balloon, and a card
that read:

> *Mother,*
>
> *We wish there was some way to show you
> how much we love you ... besides doing dish-
> es, that is. Happy Mother's Day! Love, Chris
> and Todd*

I had hoped for a relaxing breakfast in bed like
the girls used to fix, but they have both gone on to
lives of their own. Their phone call just wasn't the
same as hearing them clanging pans in the kitchen,
making my favorite blueberry coffeecake. Mother's
Day was different without them.

And kind of sad.

My husband and sons offered to take me out for
breakfast. The local restaurant was giving away pink
carnations to all mothers. I was relieved that the men
in my life didn't try to make breakfast themselves; it
would have taken me the rest of the day to clean up
the mess. I ordered blueberry pancakes.

A nice-looking family with three young daughters came in and took the table next to ours. The little
girls were dressed in lace and shiny white shoes and
their hair was in pigtails and bows. The hole in my
family got bigger, and I missed my own girls more

than ever. Well, at least the boys were trying.

The man took his seat and opened the menu while the woman found a high chair for her youngest. He read the Sunday sports section while she put a bib on the baby and fed her cereal and peaches from a jar.

While he read the funnies, she took the 4-year-old to the bathroom. He diligently ate his bacon and eggs while she buttered and cut French toast. She cleaned up spilled orange juice while he sipped a second cup of coffee. Her first cup was cold and untouched.

As he folded the newspaper, she dipped a corner of her napkin in a glass of water and cleaned the face of the baby, who was now seated in her lap. She took an extra moment to clean a bit of food off her blouse.

As he paid the check, she gathered up bottles, bibs, and baby food and put jackets on her little brood.

"Are you ready?" the man asked, unwrapping a mint.

"Yes, dear. Thank you. What a relaxing morning … and no dishes to wash!"

As we rose to leave, I glanced at the messy table next to ours. A hair ribbon and the pink carnation lay forgotten among the plates of half-eaten French toast.

The lady was right, no dishes to wash.

The blueberry pancakes were delicious. As I looked forward to spending the rest of the day curled up with a good book, I realized that maybe the phone call was enough after all!

Prayer

Thanks, Lord, for my family. Amen.

The Blue-Jeaned Ballplayer

Do not wear yourself out to get rich;
have the wisdom to show restraint.
Proverbs 23:4

This baseball strike really makes me mad. My young son is devastated that he can't see his favorite players on TV anymore. We promised to take him to a Rockies game, but it was canceled.

I wish the greedy adults could remember what it was like to be in Little League. My second grader plays in blue jeans and sneakers. He slides into first base, not because he's supposed to, but "cuz it's fun!" to slide. He takes a toy car into the outfield with him to have something to do. No one can hit the ball that far. And when he bats, he jumps for joy when he finally hits the ball, forgetting to run. He doesn't care as much about winning as getting to play catcher. That's the best position.

I wonder why there aren't professional baseball teams for women. I can't imagine any woman I know complaining about getting a "measly" million dollars for playing any kind of game. Women are much too smart for that. I think most of us would just be glad to play. Maybe it's time to let the women take the field. But then again, most of us would refuse to wear those uniforms.

Prayer

Lord, provide godly heroes for the young blue-jeaned ballplayers. Help us set good examples for our children. May we instill in our family members the importance of good sportsmanship. Instead of greed, lead us to crave a deeper relationship with You and with those around us. Through our actions, may we witness our faith in Jesus. For His sake, forgive us for the times we make worldly wealth more important that spiritual wealth. In Jesus' name. Amen.

SECTION 3

FEASTING WITH STRIFE

Don't Let Go!

When I said, "My foot is slipping," Your love, O Lord, supported me. *Psalm 94:18*

One day when she was 3 years old, I started to dress her. "I can do it all by meself!" she announced. I still had to do the buttons.

On her first day of kindergarten, I started to walk her to the classroom. "I can go by meself," she boldly shrilled. Just before reaching the door, the tiny steps faltered. "It's okay," I encouraged. "Go and have fun!"

When she learned to ride a bike, she excitedly cried out, "I'm riding all by myself!" Then she added, "Don't let go!"

When she was 14, I tried to help her pick out a dress for the junior high school dance. "Oh, Mother," she retorted as she rolled her eyes at me. "That one is soooo gross!" Then she asked if she could borrow my pearl earrings.

The night before she graduated from high school, she exclaimed, "Now I can finally be independent!" Then she asked if I had ironed her graduation gown.

When she was in college, she decided to open a checking account. I paid the overdraft.

Now she is in love. She wants to get married. She's pregnant. Where did my little girl go?

Prayer

Heavenly Father, You have given me the strength to handle the many struggles of motherhood. But don't let go yet! In Your Son's name. Amen.

The War Zone

Better a dry crust with peace and quiet
than a house full of feasting, with strife.
Proverbs 17:1

Why do my children fight so much? We're supposed to be a family, yet they act like the bathroom is a war zone. Curling irons become sabers; blow dryers transform into machine guns. I'm fed up with the morning bickering.

Who used all the hot water? She used my toothbrush! Tell her to get out of the bathroom, she's been in there forever ... And on and on it goes.

Dinnertime is even worse. Why can't we, for once, have a dinner table like you see in a Rockwell painting? Just once I'd like to go through a meal without spilled milk, an argument over who got the biggest piece of cake, or rolled eyes from my teenager. Just once I'd like to hear someone say, "Sure, Mom, I'll be glad to do the dishes."

And while I'm dreaming, another of my children would add nicely, "Here, let me help you!"

Maybe if I use the good dishes and put a few candles on the table. Maybe if I treat everyone like dinner guests.

Prayer

Thanks, Lord. The idea worked. The kids were shocked at first, but they actually thought it was fun. No one spilled a thing. When my son passed the butter, his sister even said thank you without being sarcastic. Now what am I going to do about the bathroom? Amen.

The Sunset

Do not let the sun go down while you are still angry. *Ephesians 4:26*

What an awful argument. Why doesn't my daughter listen to me? Just because she's about to graduate from high school doesn't mean she knows everything!

Forgive me for the angry words, Lord. As I sit here on this hillside, I'm aware of Your splendor. As the sun sets, it reminds me of my daughter's childhood, which is also melting into the not-so-distant horizon. I don't know if either of us is quite ready for that. We both enjoyed the sunshine of her youth.

But wait! As I walk back towards home, a large full moon rises over the rugged mountain peaks. It illuminates the snow, exposing a thousand glittering diamonds. The pine trees glow with its light.

Yes, the sunny days of childhood will set, but in their place a glorious surprise is unfolding ... my grown-up daughter.

Prayer

Thank You, Lord, for helping me see that for every sunset there will be a sunrise. As You have walked with me and guided me through her childhood, take my hand and lead me—us—through the years of adulthood. Give us both a forgiving spirit for the time of conflict we will face. In Jesus' name. Amen.

The Compliment

He who refreshes others will himself be refreshed. *Proverbs 11:25*

"Does your daughter work at McDonald's?" the woman asked.

"Why, yes, she does," I replied.

"She gave me the best service the other day and was extremely polite. You must have raised her right!"

Just those few sentences. Nothing fancy. It only took a moment to say them. But it made my day.

It's remarkable how a few kind words about a child can make a parent beam with pride. Yes, I know she's a "go-getter." I know she takes pride in the job she does, even if it is making fries and handing out burgers. But hearing another adult praise her work made the job she does even more special.

Lord, the next time I see someone else's child do a good job or a good deed, help me remember how much this woman's words brightened my day. We parents, especially the parents of teenagers, need to hear that others appreciate our kids as much as we do. Words from the "outside" can refresh and encourage.

Prayer

Lord, help us all as parents. Guide our words and actions so that we may build our children up and not tear them down. When we hear praise from friends or even strangers, remind us to pass that praise along to our children. Thank You for the gift of Your Son, whose loving sacrifice sets the example of true service. Let our actions always reflect His presence in our lives. In Jesus' name. Amen.

The Me-Attitude

Serve one another in love. *Galatians 5:13*

When I was a teenager, I don't remember having such a me-attitude. I didn't think my whole family revolved around me. Dad never paid child support so Mom couldn't give me a lot. Somehow I knew she was doing all she could, and I don't recall having the you-owe-me attitude my daughter has.

Or did I? I resented Mom because she couldn't

pay for my cheerleading uniform. I had to save my waitressing tips instead. My best friend got a new car for her 16th birthday; I got seat covers for an old junker.

I resented Mom because she wasn't there when I was sick with the stomach flu. I called her at work, but she couldn't come home. I'll never forget how scared I was. I hated the fact that she worked two jobs, and I had to do all the cleaning.

I guess I had a me-attitude after all.

Prayer

You know, Lord, it's funny that in the last few years the resentment I felt about my childhood has turned to admiration. Come to think of it, the turnaround started about the time my own daughter became a teenager. Help my daughter and me communicate our feelings. Thank You for not placing Yourself first. Instead of a me-attitude, You came to earth as a servant and humbly went to the cross for my sins. Through You, I have forgiveness and eternal life. Help me share these precious gifts with my daughter. In Jesus' name. Amen.

The Drill Sergeant

No discipline seems pleasant at the time.
... Later on, however, it produces a harvest
of righteousness and peace. *Hebrews 12:11*

Pick up your clothes. Put that away.
Your hair is so dirty. Wash it today.

Your room is a mess. Your homework's not done.
There's more to this life than just having fun.

Your hair isn't right; your clothes, a disgrace.
And take some of that makeup off of your face.

Do I have to keep saying over and over,
"Listen to me!" "Be nice to your brother!"?

If I've told you once, I've told you twice
I said your hair still isn't right.

Did you clean up the bathroom or leave it a mess?
Did you take out the trash and study for the test?

I tell you and tell you, and still you don't hear,
Turn down the music, you'll ruin your ears!

Can't you do anything without being told?
Put on your coat. Wrap up. You'll catch cold.

I'm not being unfair, you know that it's true,
I only say it because I love you!

Prayer

Dear Jesus, sometimes it seems like my days are filled with litanies of dos and don'ts. If I feel that way, how must my kids feel? As I set the rules, remind me to keep them in agreement with Your rules. Help me express to my kids the love that underlies my requests. Give all of us an obedient spirit and a forgiving heart. Remind us that You have set us free from the bonds of the Law so that we may joyfully obey and serve others. In Your name. Amen.

Every Woman Needs Her Own Room

By wisdom a house is built, and through understanding it is established; through knowledge its rooms are filled with rare and beautiful treasures. *Proverbs 24:3–4*

When my daughter graduated from high school and moved out, my two younger sons flipped a coin to see who would get her bedroom. They both lost.

I called heads *and* tails.

My old Raggedy Ann keeps my daughter's bear company on the silky apricot bedspread. Two king-size pillows at the head of the antique iron bed make the room a welcome place. They beg someone to snuggle into them and read. The afghan that Aunt Brenda made drapes across the foot of the bed. It's just the right weight for a mid-afternoon nap.

My favorite books line the shelf next to the old radio, which is set to my music station. A wicker basket once filled with *Seventeen* now holds *Better Homes and Gardens*. African violets have a new home on the eastern windowsill and thrive with the right amount of sun.

A few of my daughter's childhood treasures remain. Tiny pink ballet slippers hang on the mirror. Stuffed animals are piled in the corner. My newly remodeled retreat would be a little too empty without them.

The ribbons and high school mementos on the

bulletin board now share the space with nifty motherly sayings collected over the past 18 years. One in the center was read often on late nights, "I gave you life … but cannot live it for you." My inner alarm clock still goes off at midnight.

The desk once covered with algebra and chemistry homework now displays neat stacks of floral stationery and a journal. A well-worn Bible lies on the dresser next to the bed, another late-night necessity when the room feels too empty.

Maybe this really isn't my room after all. I share it with memories that aren't quite ready to be packed away.

Prayer

Lord, I know it's a bit selfish of me to turn this room into my own retreat. My sons need their own rooms too. They're getting too big for their bunk beds. But for now I thank You for this room and for all the many treasures it holds. Thank You for this small place where I can hear an echo of giggling girls when my nest feels vacant and bare. I'm just not quite ready to remodel completely. In Jesus' name. Amen.

You Are So Unfair!

Provide your slaves with what is right and fair, because you know that you also have a Master in heaven. *Colossians 4:1*

The other night, my daughter asked to go to a party. I asked the usual questions, "Who will be there? Are the parents going to be home? Is your homework done? And the dishes?"

I got evasive answers. "Home by 11," I commanded.

"But Mother, all the other kids get to stay out until ..."

"Eleven. And that's final."

"Why do you do this to me? You are so unfair!"

My mind drifted back to another place and time. How many times had I heard those same words, "That's final." How many times did I think my mother was unfair, that I was poor Cinderella and she was the wicked stepmother?

I remember vowing never to be like my mom when I had children. And now I sound just like my mother.

Now I'm the unfair master and my children are my slaves. Slaves to my beliefs and worries, they're bound in the chains of what I feel is right for them.

In some ways, I'm still a slave to my maternal master. I sometimes still think I need to please her or that she's unfair. I'm bound by the chains she lovingly wrapped around me: my faith in God, His rules of right and wrong, and the need to do what's right for our children.

Prayer

Loving Master, sometimes I think You are unfair. Sometimes I feel my prayers go unanswered. I pray for freedom from the bondage of jobs, kids, and commitments, but the chains remain. Many times I argue with You, but You firmly say, "That's final." But blest be the tie that binds. Through Jesus' death and resurrection, I am bound to You. The chains of love are firmly in place. In You I have strength and encouragement for the times the bonds of earth begin to strangle. Your yoke of grace is really a precious freedom. It is an anchor that keeps my tiny boat stable in the sometimes angry sea of motherhood. Thank You for paying the price to make me Yours. In Jesus' name. Amen.

Onward, Christian Soldiers

Before the rooster crows, you will disown
Me three times. *Matthew 26:75*

My daughter had to write a paper for her high school English class. She chose the topic "Vietnam, 20 Years Later." I took the afternoon off from work, and we drove to the Veterans hospital to speak with a soldier who served in that war and is now a counselor.

The one-hour appointment stretched into three. Jake was just a couple years older than me. He told my daughter that he was only 18 when he shipped out to Vietnam, just one year older than her. My daughter's glorified Hollywood version of the war crumbled into the grim reality of what he had experienced as a medic in the foreign and torturous jungles of Nam.

And when Jake described finally getting out, a more depressing scenario unfolded. Anxious to return to the States, he was spit upon as he exited the plane in Seattle. He was forced to change into "civies" to avoid angry stares and crude curses. Memories flooded back to me as he spoke: defiant protest songs, Kent State, peace symbols, a friend who never returned.

Jake's face was dignified when, through tearful eyes, he recounted searching "The Wall" for names of buddies who never came home. They gave the ultimate sacrifice.

I expected Jake to be bitter, but he wasn't. He was proud, as proud as the soldiers who came back from World War II to banners, cheers, and parades. He had been willing to lay down his life for his country and what it stands for—the freedom of all men and women. He reminded us of the men who had fought more than 200 years ago for the freedom to worship God in their own way.

My daughter got much more from Jake than just research for an English paper. She got a lesson in love, in hate, and in true sacrifice—a lesson of standing up for your beliefs even when the world condemns you for it. It's a lesson that she—and I—will never forget.

Prayer

Lord, forgive me for the times I deny You ... for the times in the break room when I listen to the slander of religion and sit in silence, afraid of being labeled a "holy roller." Thank You for all the men and women who have sacrificed so much to protect my freedom to worship You.

Thank You for all Your mighty soldiers. Help me, Lord. Send me into battle with Your protective armor. I don't want the cock to crow again. In Jesus' name. Amen.

Not to Worry!

[Mary said,] "Son, why have You treated us like this? Your father and I have been anxiously searching for You." *Luke 2:48*

Jesus—the most perfect Son. Mary—a celebrated mother. Was she exempt from worry? Did her most-perfect Son ever cause her any stress? Just read on.

Luke 2:41–52 tells us that when Jesus was 12 years old, His family made the trip to Jerusalem for the Passover. A big celebration. A party.

When it came time to return home, Joseph and Mary were unaware that Jesus had stayed behind. Jesus, the perfect Son, never asked for permission. After traveling for a day, His parents missed Him. They asked their friends and relatives, "Have you seen Jesus?"

"No, I thought He was with you."

"Maybe He chose to ride with Zechariah."

"No, we haven't seen Him all day."

We can imagine Mary's worry. We feel her anxiety. She and Joseph rushed back to Jerusalem and searched everywhere for Jesus, combing the streets and alleyways. I doubt Mary slept. She, like any mother, probably began to fear the worst.

"This is just not like Him! He's such a fine boy; He would never worry me like this. He must be hurt. Oh, Joseph, where could He be?"

When they finally found Him in the temple courts, relief turned to astonishment as His mother said to Him, "Son, why have You treated us like this? Your father and I have been anxiously searching for You."

The young man's answer was, "Why were you searching for Me? Didn't you know I had to be in My Father's house?" (v. 49). His anxious parents did not understand Jesus. They were exhausted from worry and sleepless nights but very grateful that their Son was alive and well.

Mary did what all mothers through the ages have done. She *treasured* all these things in her heart, not just the good times but also the challenging times.

Prayer

Lord, help me treasure each moment, each day. You have given me such precious gifts—family, health, salvation. Guide my thoughts to reflect on Your presence and move me to share You in word and action with those around me. Remind me to always do Your work. In my Savior Jesus' name. Amen.

But I Want Better for You

There is surely a future hope for you, and your hope will not be cut off. *Proverbs 23:18*

I'm so disappointed. My daughter doesn't want to go to college. I had such big plans when she received the acceptance letter from a good school. I was so proud. Her future looked bright and exciting. It was the kind of future I always wanted for her.

For years I saved a little out of every paycheck. I dreamed that my daughter would experience what I never had: college life, books full of new ideas, and a chance at a high-paying job.

Instead she is choosing to work nights as a waitress. I know how tired she is—how her feet ache, her back, her neck, her head. I felt the same aches. She talks about looking for an eight-to-five job in a clothing store, even though she has no experience.

I had no experience either, but somehow I have a 14-year career in banking. I still remember how I wanted to go to college. First there wasn't money. Then there wasn't time. I was too busy working and planning my daughter's future. It's hard to let go of the plans I built for her. It's hard to see someone I love not fulfill the dreams I've had for her since she wore tiny pink booties.

How does a parent learn to say, "I love you. I will

support you and your decisions"? Lord, help me support and respect my child even though she isn't fulfilling my dreams. Make this my prayer for my daughter: that she may be happy in all that *she* does and becomes, not what I want her to be.

Instead of living my dreams through her, maybe it's time to fulfill them myself. I can use the education fund for the classes I've always wanted to take.

Prayer

Lord, thank You for giving each person unique talents and desires for the future. Help me back off and let my daughter live her own life. And help me live my own to its fullest. Thanks for sending Jesus to die and rise again for us. Through Him we have the greatest sense of worth because He has made us Your children. In Him we have hope for an unimaginably brilliant future: eternal life in heaven. In the name of Jesus. Amen.

Just Two More Years

The Lord gives wisdom, and from His mouth come knowledge and understanding. *Proverbs 2:6*

Lord, please don't let my son give up. He only has two more years of high school left. I know what a struggle it is for him. It takes him more than half an hour to type a paragraph. He miserably endures

English class while he longs to be outside tinkering on a car.

He says he feels like a prisoner in school. He wishes summer was nine months long and school only three. He loved his job as a mechanic's assistant and was so happy for those three months he was free from the chains of English grammar.

He's a good kid—kind, caring, sensitive. It hurts to see him struggle. But he needs that diploma. If he would have been born a hundred years ago, he would have quit school after eighth grade and gone to work on the family farm. But times have changed. While he probably won't need to remember the works of Edgar Allan Poe or the square root of 99, he can't get into diesel mechanics school without that piece of paper that proclaims he completed high school.

He knows every part of a tractor. He knows nothing about the parts of a sentence. Help him to be thankful for the gifts he has and not condemn himself for what he has not. Lord, give him strength and courage to stay for just two more years.

Prayer

Lord, give me wisdom to know how to help my son. Keep me from nagging and scolding. Instead, grant me understanding. Help me encourage and strengthen him. In Jesus' name. Amen.

The Good Shepherd

He tends His flock like a shepherd: He gathers the lambs in His arms and carries them close to His heart; He gently leads those that have young. *Isaiah 40:11*

I think the only thing more challenging than being a teenager is being the parent of teenagers. How do I know when to let them test their wings or when to step in and clip them? Teenagers think they know so much about this great world. One minute they seem to have no fear; the next minute they cry out against the unknown.

Even after all these years as a mother, I sometimes feel I know nothing about children, and I'm afraid too. Afraid of saying too much or of not saying enough. Please, Lord, show me the way. Guide them. And when I'm not there to lead, or they don't want to follow, please put Your angels on alert. I can't do this on my own. I can't do it with only my husband's help. I need You.

Prayer

I need Your support and Your guidance, heavenly Father. I need Your power to help me know when to ignore teenage sarcasm and when to call a halt to a friendship that may not be right. Help me know when to gather my teens into my open arms and when to gently nudge them along. Lead us all as You have promised. Bring us safely to our home with You in heaven. In Jesus' name. Amen.

Ganging Up on Gangs

> When Jesus saw this, He was indignant. He said to them, "Let the little children come to Me, and do not hinder them, for the kingdom of God belongs to such as these."
> *Mark 10:14*

There was a shooting this morning at the junior high school, and a 15-year-old child is dead. So many ugly, horrible words have entered our vocabulary like a plague. Drive-by shootings ... suicide ... violence. And the worst part is we've become immune to it.

Even in our small town, we have a gang. Kids with no direction strike out at the innocent. Our children have become victims of moral decay. They walk the halls of their schools in fear, afraid to go the bathroom alone.

They say that parents don't care anymore. They, whoever *they* are, are wrong. We do care. Not only about our own kids' lives but about the kids who aimlessly wander Main Street at midnight.

Jesus set the example—keep the kids close. Going home and fixing supper for our children is more important than going out with friends. A family vacation is more important than a weekend in Vegas. A Sunday in church is more important than a Sunday at the golf course. It's time for parents to wise up to the fact that our number one priority is not the house we live in or the car we drive.

A trip to our children's Little League games or

school plays or open houses takes precedence over a workout at the gym. Shopping sprees for designer clothes can't match the experience of doing without these expensive "extras." Kids need to learn to put value in the person, not in the clothes or shoes or accessories they wear. The high school parking lot is full of nice cars bought with parental dollars and parental guilt.

Prayer

Lord, bring Your peace to the family that's mourning the loss of their child. Give us all the courage to take back the streets and the schools. Let us be witnesses to Your saving and transforming love. Our sinfulness has been washed clean by Jesus' death, and His resurrection assures us eternal life. Send Your Spirit to guide our actions so that our children will be brought up to believe in and obey You. In Jesus' name. Amen.

Where Do I Go from Here?

The woman came and knelt before Him. "Lord, help me!" she said. *Matthew 15:25*

Where do I go from here, Lord? I don't know where she's heading. She left home in an angry rage, leaving empty drawers and empty dreams. Do I search for her or simply let her go?

I recently read a saying, "People need love the most when they deserve it the least." I still love her, God. Probably now more than ever. Please calm this terrible panic I feel deep down in my soul. Help me hold my family together during this terrible turmoil. Calm the whirlwind of fear, doubt, and guilt spinning inside my mind.

I ache for my daughter. I long to hold her in my arms and tell her how much I care. I tried but she pushed me away and said if I really cared, I would understand.

I remember what it was like to be 17 years old. I remember longing for the day I could be on my own. No rules, no parents, only freedom. But I also remember how naive and inexperienced I was.

Prayer

Lord, where do I search? Please … please help me find my daughter again. There is one place I haven't tried. Lord, I know where to go from here. Down on my knees. Protect her, Lord, and lead her back to this house. Send Your Spirit to strengthen me as I wait. I trust You to help us work through this. In Jesus' name. Amen.

Tough Love

[Jesus said,] "Love each other as I have loved you." *John 15:12*

Lord, I have nothing left to give to my daughter. She wants out. She has no desire to stay and try to work through our problems.

I'm tired of fighting. I'm tired of trying to understand her rebellious ways. I'm tired of being treated like the enemy. Maybe she's right. Maybe it is time for her to leave—time to call a truce and send her off into the real world. Experience will be the real teacher. A person who does not desire to learn by listening will have to learn by experience.

Lord, help me accept that I can't guide someone who does not choose to follow. Perhaps that takes the most courage of all … the wisdom of knowing when to let go.

Prayer

Lord, help me love my children, especially when they aren't so lovable. You loved us while we were still lost in sin. You sent Your only Son to suffer and die to redeem us. Through my Baptism, I'm buried with Jesus. And because He rose from the dead on the first Easter, I have the promise of life eternal. Because of this great love, I'm free to show love to others. Let it shine out. Work in my daughter's heart. Bring her to an understanding of how her actions affect those around her. Teach us both how to get along. In Jesus' name. Amen.

Reflections on Motherhood, Part 1

Can a mother forget the baby at her breast
and have no compassion on the child she
has borne? *Isaiah 49:15*

This is supposed to be a time of celebration. A
time to rejoice in Jesus' birth, the Son of God and of
Mary—a regular, everyday woman. "Joy to the world
... Joy ... Joy ..." The radio beckons my voice to sing
along in praise.

But I can't. Singing about a baby in a manger
only brings a heavy sadness. I wonder how Mary, a
mother like any other mother, must have felt as she
looked at her infant Son.

Did she know what was in store for that serene, soft
bundle she held so tenderly against her breast? Did she
know what despair lay ahead? Did her heart shatter as
she watched her firstborn ridiculed and tortured?

I never expected what was ahead, either. When I
held my beautiful daughter for the first time, I felt
only joy and hope. Probably the same emotions Mary
felt as she looked into baby Jesus' eyes.

And there was joy. Joy and laughter and, in my
case, Christmas pageants. I listened to giggles of antic-
ipation and saw bright, chubby red cheeks on Christmas morning. My daughter's shiny eyes beheld the
magic of Mary's Son's birth. What a present those
years were.

But now the tinsel is tarnished. The paper angel made in kindergarten is crumpled and torn from perching atop 12 Christmas trees. The wonder of Christmas has been replaced with the reality of my daughter's lost childhood.

At 18, she is going to become a mother. That's not what I had planned for her life all those years ago. But Mary probably never dreamed that her firstborn would suffer and be crucified.

How did she do it? How did she get up in the morning and plan meals? How did she go on living when her heart must have been hanging on the cross beside her Son's?

But Jesus rose again and won forgiveness and new life for Mary and for me. And for my daughter. And that gives me hope. I can trust my heavenly Father to make all this work for good. He is beside me and He will strengthen me for all that's ahead.

My heart sings, "No more shall sin and sorrow rule!"

Prayer

Heavenly Father, as much as my daughter's actions hurt me, it can never compare to the anguish Your Son felt. He was separated from You by the weight of all the world's sins—my sins, my daughter's sins, even the sins of Mary, His mother. But Jesus stuck to the plan. He accomplished the task—the cross, the death, the resurrection. I am forgiven. And so is my daughter. Focus our eyes on Jesus—our joy and our salvation. In His name. Amen.

Reflections on Motherhood, Part 2

"As a mother comforts her child, so will I comfort you," [says the Lord.] *Isaiah 66:13*

From the angel's proclamation on, Mary knew her child was special. She trusted that God had a plan for her Son. That's why even in the fog of disappointment and pain, I believe God has a plan for my daughter.

As with any mother, Mary never knew as she held her babe against her heart that the pain would hurt so much. She felt the torment as the crowds mocked Jesus. She felt the despair as He cried out, "My God, why have You forsaken Me?"

At that moment, Mary probably felt forsaken too. Her precious Son was to have been the Savior, but surrounding her that day was hatred and anger and death.

"Your will be done." How many times Mary must have used those words in prayer. But she probably beat her fists against the cold stone tomb and cried out "Why? Why didn't You stop them? Where was Your power and glory?"

But God had not forsaken Mary. And while I cannot see past the outward signs of sin's corruption, God does have a plan for my precious child. He has not left us.

The burden of a mother's love can weigh very heavy. I need to rest, be still, and know that God truly is God. He's strong enough to take my burden and carry it. He will let me curl up in the shelter of His wings.

Where is that Christmas wonder? God will give it to me again. I will see it in the eyes of my grandchild as he or she gazes in awe at the sparkling lights on the tree. I'll hear it in the innocent voice as the new baby coos to "Silent Night." I'll feel it as tiny fingers clutch mine.

When God gave Mary and me the gifts of our children, He never promised the road would be easy. His gift did not come with a written guarantee against problems. But God's gift did include a promise of support, comfort, and forgiveness. And because of Mary's child and the gift of faith in Him, we have the ultimate promise of eternal life.

God holds my hand as my daughter once held mine. He will lead her. He will lead me. Joyfully and willingly, I'll watch His plan unfold before my eyes. He will lead me back to the wonder of Christmas.

Prayer

Almighty Father, You worked a miracle in Mary's life. What a privilege and an awesome responsibility to be the mother of Your Son. But You were with her every step of the way—even in the moments of her greatest despair. My daughter is also a miracle. The privilege of raising one of Your children bears tremendous responsibility. For the times I've failed, forgive me. Send Your Spirit to strengthen me through this time of despair. I know You haven't deserted me. And I trust You will work in my daughter's life to bring about the good You have planned. In my Savior's name. Amen.

Free Spirit

His pleasure is not in the strength of the
horse, nor his delight in the legs of a man;
the Lord delights in those who fear Him,
who put their hope in His unfailing love.
Psalm 147:10–11

Riding Jazz is a commitment, not a pleasure. If I
pull the reins left, he jerks his head right. He spooks at
foxtails swaying in the breeze and bolts when walking
past a harrow.

Jazz was a beautiful foal. As I watched him rise
onto his skinny, wobbly legs and suck nourishment
from my old mare, I dreamed of the day he would
become like the proud horse in *The Black Stallion.* I
imagined us galloping through lush green meadows,
horse and rider in perfect unison.

Nothing prepared me for training this free spirit.
I learned the hard way to hang on at all times. I have
to let Jazz know who's the boss while respecting his
high spirit. His training takes understanding and
strong discipline.

Jazz reminds me of my daughter. She and I have
trouble seeing eye to eye. It's more like glare to glare.
When did the giggly, pigtailed munchkin change into
this hair-sprayed teenager? She fights the reins. She's
curious and high-spirited. Jazz kicks at the farrier. My
daughter kicks when I try to help her pick out a prom
dress. Jazz threw his head, and I had to use a tie-down.
My daughter broke curfew, and I had to ground her.

She furiously fights against the rules I set to keep her going the right way.

Prayer

Lord, help me respect the high spirit of the young. Give me strength to pull them up short when they need discipline. Help me train without crushing their vibrant spirit with a heavy hand. Remind me that I fight against You just as my daughter fights against me. Thank You for sending Jesus to suffer, die, and rise again. Through Your gift of faith in Him, my rebellious ways are forgiven. Bring us all safely to You in heaven. In Jesus' name. Amen.

When the Battle Seems Lost

With God all things are possible.
Matthew 19:26

I saw him again today, stumbling along the sidewalk. My heart aches for the parents of this wayward son. Just a few years ago, we cheered beside them in the bleachers as he confidently threw winning touchdowns. He was bright and alive; his parents were proud.

Now he throws down drinks as if there were no tomorrow. His once-proud parents grieve. They mortgaged their house to bail him out of his latest skirmish. I think they too must feel like the battle's lost.

Please give these parents strength, Lord. Help their troubled son fight his battle with booze, a hard-hitting, rough opponent.

Help us as we rally around his parents. Put the right words in our mouths to give them courage and hope. You have promised to work through all things for good—reveal the good in this situation.

Prayer

Please, God, remind us, especially these parents, that nothing is impossible for You. In Your Son's name. Amen.

The Graduation Gift

The Lord ... will watch over your life; the Lord will watch over your coming and going. *Psalm 121:7–8*

Lord, thank You for this special vacation with my daughter. We had such a wonderful time. The trip probably wasn't practical. There were so many other things she needed for graduation: a better car, some new clothes, or a good set of luggage. The cost of the trip would have paid for a whole semester of college.

We laid on the beach, snorkeled, gathered seashells, ate turtle, and talked late into the night. For once, we weren't mother and daughter. We weren't traveling companions. We were friends.

As the plane brings us back to the real world, help us bring back more than sand and suntans and keep more than the T-shirts and trinkets.

Father, help us treasure the friendship that we found on our vacation, to hold it close and listen to it as we did the seashells.

Soon my daughter will leave in a new direction. It's time for her to travel on without me. Watch over us as we go our separate ways and reunite us often.

Prayer

Thank You, Lord, for the treasured gift of my daughter ... my friend. Watch over us. Guide us. Bring us together often. In Jesus' name. Amen.

The Harvest

Then the land will yield its harvest, and
God, our God, will bless us. *Psalm 67:6*

I walk in the crisp autumn air, shuffling my feet through the crimson and gold leaves that cover the earth. I gather some to put in Gramma's cranberry colored vase.

The chipmunks scurry up the oak trees, gathering the last of the acorns. No frolicking today. They sense that winter is near as they hastily run from tree to tree.

I walk to the garden. The leaves are curled and black from frost. I've already tucked away bright orange pumpkins, green and yellow acorn squash, and tangerine carrots in the cellar.

The harvest is over, the garden ready to be tilled under for a winter's rest. Hard work, fertile soil, and God's touch have produced a crop more abundant than I imagined.

"Thank You, Lord," I whisper as I look to the mountains dusted with snow.

I pick up my daughter's old leather basketball from behind the lilac tree. She's left it behind for college. All the nurturing, weeding, praying, tender care, and God's touch has brought forth a bounty much greater than I could have ever hoped for. I hug the ball to my breast and again give thanks.

Like the great oak trees, the garden plants, and the scurrying chipmunks, I'm tired and ready for a winter's rest. The firewood is piled and the cellar stocked. My daughter is strong and healthy and ready to face the storms of life. It's been a long growing season.

The harvest is over.

I wander back to the house, light a fire, and brew a pot of spiced tea. I huddle under a warm afghan just as the snow begins to swirl around the windowpane. I pull a magazine from the rack by the chair to do some long overdue reading. It's a seed catalog.

Time to begin planning for spring.

Prayer

Thanks, Lord, for Your faithfulness and never-ending love. You supply all we need in life. I trust You to guide me as I prepare for a new season of my life. Be with my daughter as well. I place our lives in Your hands in Jesus' name. Amen.

SECTION 4

MY BEST FRIEND

My Best Friend

A friend loves at all times. *Proverbs 17:17*

Thanks for last night, Lord. Thank You for helping me find my best friend again. I thought I'd lost him. We hadn't sat and talked for so long. Somehow during the last year, we've both been so caught up in parenting, jobs, bills, and the everyday stresses that we lost sight of each other. But last night, as we talked until after midnight, I realized how much I have missed him. I have been lonely, even in a house full of family.

I never meant to shut him out. I don't really know when it started happening, probably somewhere between changing diapers and coping with teenagers. Our routines left little time for one another.

My best friend has been gone a long time even though we've been living under the same roof. A few times I thought about writing him a letter and putting S.W.A.K. on the envelope like I used to. But there was no time, even for that.

Prayer

Lord, help us take time out of our busy schedules for each other. I need my best friend. And he needs me. Now that we have our friendship back, help us take care of it.

Remind us often that You have given us to each other—to have and to hold for a lifetime. Thanks! In our Savior's name. Amen.

The Miracle Mother-in-Law

Your people will be my people and your God my God. *Ruth 1:16*

The miracle mother-in-law would welcome her new daughter into the family with open arms. She would never give advice. She would only say kind things about her son's wife, both to her face and behind her back.

She would give her daughter-in-law a present when her grandson is born. She would shower her step-grandchildren with the same love that she gives her "real" ones. She would be the most enthusiastic fan at her grandchildren's sports games.

The miracle mother-in-law would be a working woman. That way, when she walks through the front door, she would only give the unfolded clothes in the middle of the floor an understanding glance, not a critical stare.

She would make terrific potato salad and always offer to bring it to family dinners. She would do the dishes but never offer to put them away. This would save her daughter-in-law the embarrassment of watching her mother-in-law struggle to find a spot for the cutting board in the cluttered cupboards.

The miracle mother-in-law would be caring and sensitive, never bossy. She would lend a sympathetic ear in times of turmoil. Her laughter would brighten even the darkest room.

Miracles do come true. Thank you, Shirley, for being a wonderful miracle.

Prayer

Lord, some words have developed powerful negative images. Mother-in-law *is such a word. Thank You for destroying that image by putting such a wonderful woman in my life. You truly look out for Your children and supply them with people to strengthen and uplift them on their earthly walk. Keep us in Your watchful gaze and let me return as much joy to my miracle mother-in-law as she gives to me. In our Savior's name. Amen.*

PMS—Pretty Macho Syndrome

[The Sovereign Lord says,] "You are a man and not a god, though you think you are as wise as a god." *Ezekiel 28:2*

Who says only women have PMS? Men have it

too, only it's a little different—Pretty Macho Syndrome.

You might notice it when the sockets in the wrench set aren't put back in proper order. His neck will begin to turn red. Other symptoms of Pretty Macho Syndrome include throwing tools and baseball bats, stomping, kicking tires, yelling at the referee, and the famous squint-eyed glare.

The following list contains only a select few causes of male PMS:

- Toilet paper "installed" backwards
- Too much chatter at the dinner table
- Clothes put away inside out, especially socks
- The Yankees losing
- Lousy umpires
- Talking while hunting
- Another fisherman in *his* spot (especially if the fisher*man* is a fisher*woman*!)
- An overheated engine
- Litter boxes

It's too bad some company hasn't developed a pill for Pretty Macho Syndrome. It would make a fortune. Personally, I would buy a year's supply and during football season mix it into the onion dip.

Prayer

Lord, give me patience and understanding when it comes to my husband. Sometimes I forget all the pressures on him as father, husband, employee, and friend. Just as I demand my "space," I need to give him a chance to be his own person. Help me respect his requests and accommodate his idiosyncrasies. Lead us both to dependence on You for the strength to forgive. Give us Your Spirit to bind us more closely together. In Jesus' name. Amen.

Salt and Pepper

So they are no longer two, but one.
Mark 10:8

Dear Lord, love is such a mystery. How in the world did You ever bring my husband and me together?

He was a bachelor. I was a widow with three children.

He loves horses. I love cats.

He loves football. I love to read.

He is rock solid. I jump in with both feet before testing the water.

He reads the instructions. I always have a few screws left over.

He finds You in the beauty of the mountains. I find You in a quiet church.

His faith never falters. I sometimes question why.

He is the salt of the earth. I am pepper and pizazz.

Prayer

Thank You, heavenly Father, for brilliantly matching

us together. We, like salt and pepper, are a matched set—different, yet a part of each other. And through Your infinite goodness, we are one. In Jesus' name. Amen.

The Mating Game

May you rejoice in the wife of your youth.
Proverbs 5:18

My husband and I went to my son's high school for a dinner. Parents were invited to stay for the dance that followed, but my husband and I were tired. We wanted to go home and watch the Olympics. I really didn't think my son would want us there anyway.

He's old enough that parents aren't cool. He, like most of the other kids, had chosen to sit with the pack—parents on one side of the room, kids on the other.

I couldn't help staring as the young teens interacted. Cocky attitudes prevailed as the boys tried stupid antics, like balancing a spoon on their noses, to impress the girls. Some of the girls giggled while others pursued prospective dates more openly. The whole scene reminded me of a peacock mating ritual where the males proudly swagger with colorful feathers and the females dance around them.

My husband doesn't try very hard to impress me anymore. Nor I him. Instead, we contentedly lounge around in our sweats, hair uncombed. Once in a while, my mate tries to split a piece of wood that is much too large. I tell him to be careful; he might get a hernia.

Sometimes I still try to impress him with a cute nightie instead of a T-shirt, or some fancy gourmet dish out of *Bon Appetit* instead of tuna casserole. But usually, the ritual takes too much energy and we're tired. We'd much rather sit out a turn and watch TV or read a book.

I guess we both feel that we've already won the game.

Prayer

Thank You, Lord, for the comfortable relationship I share with my husband. You have brought us together as friends and so much more. We don't need to "play" the game. Help us seek Your will for our marriage. Strengthen our faith in You and our commitment to You and to each other. Send us Your Spirit and instill in us forgiving attitudes. In Your Son's name we ask this. Amen.

Marital Arts

Bear with each other and forgive whatever grievances you may have against one another. *Colossians 3:13*

The questionnaire asked for my martial status: S, M, D, or W.

Oh ... it wanted my *marital* status. I circled M.

It was no wonder I misread the word. Just this morning, martial law had been declared in our house. Martial law is temporary jurisdiction or rule by military forces over citizens of an area where civil law no longer functions or exists.

My husband had become the five-star general, and I was ready to commit treason. All previous rule, civility, and duty rosters are thrown out when you help him clean the garage. He gets stubborn and demanding. He barks orders, and the kids and I are expected to snap to attention. Fall in and listen up!

But my son wanted to shoot hoops before he put the ball away. And my teenage daughter needed to put her makeup on first. I couldn't bring myself to throw away last year's potting soil or the little plastic gizmos the petunias came in, even though he told me in his most commanding voice that I didn't need them.

The final blow came when I threw away the General's old football jersey, which I recently had given my son to use for a grease rag. We both received a quick and hasty court martial from the General. The rest of the kids ran for cover from his artillery. Even the dog made a hasty retreat.

I slammed the door on my way into the house. Fine! He could just fight his own battle, conquer the workbench by himself. I hoped the cobwebs would sabotage him.

The General arrived later, battle weary and scarred with dirt and grime. He had fought a good fight and defeated the brigade of clutter in the garage.

He may know martial law, but I know marital

arts. I can win him over any time with my own gentle strategy—a sort of sneak attack. I soothed the warrior with some TLC. I praised him for organizing the gardening tools and patted my fellow comrade on the back for sorting the screws into baby food jars.

When I knew he was sound asleep in the recliner, I tiptoed to the trash can and retrieved the oily football jersey ... and the petunia gizmos.

Ah, the spoils of war!

Prayer

Help me bear with my husband, Lord, and forgive our petty arguments. In Your Son's name. Amen.

The Wicked Stepparent

Fathers ... bring [children] up in the training and instruction of the Lord. *Ephesians 6:4*

I'm thankful my husband did not have kids when he married me. I don't think I could have put up with all he's had to face with my kids. How many times has he heard, "You aren't my dad so don't think you can tell me what to do!"? My children often accuse him of trying to take their father's place.

Stepparenting is a thankless job. Stepparents get all the work and heartache of raising children and none of the credit. They are the Rodney Dangerfields of parenting—they get no respect. Stepfathers work hard to provide shelter and security, then watch the children run into the gift-filled arms of their birth fathers. Stepmothers clean up after the stomach flu but are condemned for the spaghetti that doesn't taste like "my mom's."

I can be as guilty as my kids. Sometimes I ruffle my motherly feathers when my husband tries to discipline the kids. At times I still think of them as "my" kids, even though he has helped raise them for more than 10 years.

Stepparents have the *option* of taking on the responsibility of someone else's children. Instead of receiving praise for asking to be a part of children's lives, they become the cause of what goes wrong. There's no credit for "stepping in," no glory for coaching games, no rewards for attending fifth-grade band concerts or giving up golf for Little League.

Prayer

Lord, give an extra dose of love and patience to stepparents, to the people who do the awesome job of raising someone else's children. To the caring people who seldom get the credit, or the thank you, give an extra measure of strength. Instill in children and parents respect for each other, whether "steps" or not. Your Son came to earth and had a "stepfather." Joseph saw to all His earthly needs—and no doubt loved Jesus as his own. And You, Lord, have made us Your children through faith in Jesus. Let us rejoice in this gift and the gift of parents and stepparents who love us. In Jesus' name. Amen.

Too Tired for Love

Give us today our daily bread. *Matthew 6:11*

He wants a kiss. I'm busy fixing dinner. He wants to tell me about his bad day. I don't want to hear about it. I had one of my own. He beckons me to sit down beside him. I have to help one of the kids with a science report. He pulls me close in bed and wants to cuddle. I want to turn over and snuggle my pillow.

I'm just too tired for love tonight. I don't want it. And I don't have any left to give back. I roll over and pretend to be asleep. It's a relief to hear him get up and go into the living room to watch the news.

What's wrong with me, God? I know I'm burning the candle at both ends. Before long, I will burn out completely. But what do I give up? The kids need me, my job needs me, my mother needs me.

He needs me too. But I have poured out so much love lately that I feel totally drained. I have nothing left to give. I'm sorry for ignoring him. I love him, but I don't have the energy to show it. I know he's hurt and that he thinks I put everything in my life before him.

And sadly, sometimes he's right. My job demands so much of me. And the kids demand the rest. All he gets are the leftovers, but there's nothing left on the plate.

Prayer

Lord, my husband is hungry for a hug. All he wants

is a small gesture of my love for him: a kind word, a gentle smile, or a touch of my hand. As I nourish all the love-hungry people in my life, remind me constantly to nourish my husband. You have brought us together to support one another. Grant us trust in Your will for this relationship. Give us the energy to show each other how important the relationship is. Forgive our inability to prioritize our lives correctly. Guide our efforts. Let love be our motivation. In Jesus' name. Amen.

A Warm Cup of Love

Love each other as I have loved you.
John 15:12

Last year my husband gave me flowers for Valentine's Day. The roses and carnations came in a coffee mug that had "You Are Special" scrolled on the front in lacy pink lettering. After the flowers wilted, I threw them in the trash and kept the pink bow in my treasure box.

Every morning for the past year, the coffee mug has been full of amber liquid and sitting on the nightstand when I wake up. The aroma gently nudged me away from my dreams. Usually my husband was already dressed and gone, and many times the coffee was cold. But I knew he'd been there. I knew he had stood beside the bed and whispered "I love you" as he placed the warm cup of love beside me.

Despite quarrels or angry words the night before, my husband's special cup of love waited to greet me the next morning. There was a cup waiting after I spent half the night worrying about one of the kids. There was a cup waiting after a night spent crying over a family crisis. There was a cup waiting even after he spent the night on the couch.

The beautiful roses and carnations are long gone. The pink ribbon faded, and the cup has a chip in it. But the real gift has bloomed every morning—"You Are Special." And the best gift of all is knowing I have been loved for a whole year, not only on the good days but also on the bad. I've been loved not only when I felt I deserved it but on the days I didn't feel special at all.

I probably didn't always look beautiful or worthy of his love as my husband placed that cup beside the bed. On some mornings he probably wanted to put salt in my cup or just forget the whole thing.

But he brought me a cup of love anyway.

Prayer

Lord, thank You for this warm cup that overflows with the joy of a whole year of unconditional love. It is a treasure beyond measure. In Your name. Amen.

Stubborn!

*You then, my son, be strong in the grace
that is in Christ Jesus. 2 Timothy 2:1*

Sometimes that husband of mine is so darn stubborn and set in his ways! He won't eat anything that has peas in it. He won't consider buying anything but a Ford. He wouldn't be caught dead in shorts. And he won't leave the house without either a ball cap or his cowboy hat.

He refuses to try anything new. Sometimes that unyielding "my way is the right way" attitude makes me want to wring his neck. Once I made quiche; he thought it was awful. The next time I made it, I left out the broccoli and called it "cowboy pie." He ate the whole thing.

Yesterday at the Fourth of July parade, we sat on the left side of the street by the Texaco station. We always sit there. We were having a nice conversation with the neighbors when the flag went by. He stopped in mid-sentence, took off his hat, and put it over his heart. Never said anything, just did it.

No, he is not a veteran. He has never served in any war. He did it because he respects the flag and all that it stands for. Our young son looked up at his father and he too took off his little blue ball cap and placed it over his heart.

Maybe this same stubbornness brings us to the same pew every Sunday at 8 a.m. Maybe this same stubbornness calls us back to the table after dinner every night for devotions. I know this same stubbornness is really one of his best traits.

Prayer

Lord, thank You for this man who is teaching his son that morals do not bend. Thank You for this strong-minded man who still believes in God and country. You brought such gifts to my life, including someone who places You first in His life. In Jesus' name. Amen.

The Insult

If an enemy were insulting me, I could endure it; if a foe were raising himself against me, I could hide from him. But it is you, a man like myself, my companion, my close friend. *Psalm 55:12–13*

His words have hurt me clear to my soul. I know he had a bad day, but he didn't have to take it out on me. His rudeness hurts, God. He's supposed to be my friend.

I know I should forgive his angry outburst. He said he was sorry, even brought me a bouquet of daisies. But I can still hear the words. I can't make them go away. I wish I could.

I'm terribly alone. I miss my friend. I lay beside him in bed and pull the blankets, and the hurt, around me like a cocoon. He reaches out to me, but I move closer to the edge. I just can't face him right now.

God, there are two words that are very hard to say ... I'm sorry.

But there are three that are even harder to say ... You are forgiven.

Prayer

Dear Lord, I get angry. I say things I wish I hadn't. I insult my husband too. Worse yet, each action is a rebellion against You. I push You away when I try to deal with matters on my own. I refuse to ask for Your forgiveness when I refuse to offer it to others. Forgive me, Lord, for Jesus' sake. He forgave even those who nailed Him to the cross. Mold me into Christ's image. Make me a forgiving servant. Guide me now as I wake my husband and forgive him and ask his forgiveness as well. In my Savior's name. Amen.

Laid Off

May the favor of the Lord our God rest upon us; establish the work of our hands for us—yes, establish the work of our hands. *Psalm 90:17*

How could this happen? After nine years with the company, my husband lost his job. I'm terrified. We can't live on my salary alone, and now we have no health insurance.

How are the bills going to get paid? We still owe on the girls' braces, and then there's house payments, car payments, electricity, and the phone. My check will never stretch to cover it all.

But I'm more worried about my husband's lack of confidence. He lost more than a job—he lost his pride. Every day he sends out resumés and goes to job interviews but comes up empty.

And he never laughs anymore.

He tries to fill his empty days by "helping" me around the house. Last week he ruined my favorite silk blouse. He rearranged my kitchen cupboards, and I can't find a thing. He gripes at the kids for not being responsible, but I think it's really that he doesn't feel responsible anymore. I wish I could tell him how scared I am, but it would be a low blow to his already weak ego.

But we are family. Good times and bad. Help us stick together, Lord.

Prayer

Lord, give me patience with my husband. Strengthen my trust that You will get us through this difficult time. I know that when one door closes another will eventually open. Give us Your security in this very insecure time. Let us learn from this new challenge, be grateful for all that we have, and avoid dwelling on what we have lost. You have already given us so much—each other, our unique abilities, our home, our minds, and most important, our faith. And no matter what happens here on earth, we have the hope of new life with You in heaven. In Jesus' name. Amen.

Moving On

Surely goodness and love will follow me
all the days of my life, and I will dwell in
the house of the Lord forever. *Psalm 23:6*

I never thought "whither thou goest" would be
so hard. As I take baby pictures off the wall and wrap
them in newspaper, the black ink that stains my
hands stains my heart. I remember hanging these pictures 10 years ago. I vowed never to take them down
again, yet down they come, leaving only a nail and a
bare square in the paint.

I moved here when my daughter was a giggling
second grader. Just last month we celebrated her graduation. Now it is time for both of us to move on.

This old house has been a warm and comforting
fortress. No matter what storms of life pounded down,
this house was a port. It was home. Suddenly I am
casting off into an unknown sea, away from my
secure surroundings.

The willow tree was just a spike in the ground
when we moved in. Now it is strong and stately, providing cool shade in the front yard. The rose bushes
along the back fence have set down deep roots and
bloom profusely. Will the new owners take care of
them? I must remember to tell them to spray for
aphids.

I am being yanked up by the roots ... transplant-
ed. Will I bloom again, God?

I know it's time to break out of this safe haven,

but as I pack the last of our memories into this flimsy cardboard box, I can't help but feel an echoing emptiness. How I will miss the quiet mornings spent reading in the sunroom. The new house doesn't have one. I'll miss the smell of lavender as I hang out the clothes. I'll miss the marks on the wall where I measured my growing family. I'll miss the sound of the water pipes and the squeaky floorboard in the hall.

Prayer

Please Father, help me adjust to this move—to find the new light switches and to remember the faucet in the bathroom has the hot and cold reversed. Help me remember that comfort and security does not come from four walls ... it comes from You. In Jesus' name. Amen.

The Loose Nut behind the Wheel

A wise man listens to advice. *Proverbs 12:15*

I told my husband the car was making a funny noise—kind of a *k-chink, kaaachkinnk.* He thought I must have been listening to loony tunes on the radio. He gave me one of those "loose nut" looks and advised that it was probably just a rock in the hubcap. The noise continued to get louder and I complained again. Now it sounded more like a *kachinkachinkaaa.*

"Take it to the mechanic tomorrow," he advised, not really listening.

I think all men must practice that "loose nut" look in the mirror. The mechanic has his down pat but adds a rolled-eye sigh. It must be why he charged so much. "Just a loose bolt in the whatschama-gimme," he said as he greedily pocketed the check.

The *kachink* turned to a *kachunk,* and I complained again. No way was I taking it back, I retorted. Didn't my husband remember the contract he signed on our wedding day? The fine print between the lines said that he was in charge of all the greasy stuff. He must have forgotten.

Now he is calling me from a diner out on Highway 50. This time he was the loose nut behind the wheel. He said the car went *kachink, kachunk* … just before it went kaput!

Prayer

Lord, help us listen to one another in love. Amen.

Just for Tonight

Love each other. *John 15:12*

Just for tonight, Lord, let me put my worries aside and concentrate on his.

Just for tonight, let me rub his back and give him the attention he needs.

Just for tonight, let me hear his voice ... not the kids' or my mother's or my friend on the phone.

Just for tonight, let me not wonder if the doors are locked or if there are still clothes in the washer.

Just for tonight, let me focus my love on him.

Prayer

Father, sometimes I get so caught up in everything else that I neglect this wonderful man. I become selfish and demand his attention but rarely do I concentrate on giving him mine. Strengthen our love for one another and keep us ever willing to share our lives and listen to each other. Let us love as You have loved us. In Jesus' name. Amen.

Does Superwoman Take Vitamins?

No Warranty

Your body is a temple of the Holy Spirit. ...
Honor God with your body. *1 Corinthians
6:19–20*

Lord, I don't feel pretty anymore. I want shiny
hair, but coloring has left it drab and lifeless, just like
the rest of my body. I want to look like I did in my 20s:
a tight, flat tummy and a strong, vibrant body. They
say real beauty comes from the inside. Maybe that's
my problem, I don't feel beautiful on the inside. I feel
sluggish and cluttered.

When my car began to misfire, I took it to the
garage. The mechanic changed the oil, put in new
antifreeze, gave it a lube job, and installed new spark
plugs. It ran so well that I took it to a body shop and
had the dents pounded out and the rust spots painted.
After a good wax job, the old car looked as good as
new.

That's what I need, an overhaul. A new set of
plugs to add some spark to my mundane, sluggish life.
A body shop to massage out the kinks in my neck. A
facial to ease the fine lines forming around my eyes.
And maybe a paint job to help me feel shiny and new.

I would love to take a vacation at a health spa,
but I can't afford that kind of body shop. What I need

is a major do-it-yourself overhaul. I could take a couple days off or even a weekend. A hot oil treatment and a new cut would bring out the curl in my hair. A long soak in a bubble bath and a loofah sponge would rub away my dry winter skin. If I soaked my feet in Epsom salts and worked on the callouses caused from running in high heels, my feet might not feel so tired. Then I'd be more willing to spend money to replace the balding tires I've been wearing. A cucumber mask would lighten up these dark circles, and a body oil could massage away the knots in my muscles. A long walk in the fresh air would clean out my clogged carburetor and drinking juice instead of coffee would clean out my radiator.

I need two days in my body shop to pamper, tighten, scrub, and massage this old carriage. Then maybe it will be ready for another five years or 50,000 miles. Too bad there isn't a warranty.

No, that's good. All the more reason to take care of this body. It's the only one I've got.

Prayer

Lord, thank You for this spark plug of an idea, this maintenance plan. Cars can be replaced, but I will have this body for a lifetime. Thank You for just enough spark of vanity to realize how important it is to take care of me. Thanks for the health You have given me thus far, and keep me running well until You call me home. In Jesus' name. Amen.

Calling in Sick

I am the Lord, who heals you. *Exodus 15:26*

I called in sick today. My joints ache and my head feels like a water balloon ready to explode. Even my fingernails hurt. So why do I feel like a kid playing hooky from school?

Someone else will have to finish the report. Someone else will have to answer my phone. Someone else will have to do my filing. My co-workers are overloaded already. I feel guilty.

If I bake cookies for them, they will think I wasn't really sick at all. I don't feel well enough to do it anyway. Maybe I should just take a nap and go in at noon. But the warm blanket feels so good. The hot tea soothes my raw, sore throat.

The house is quiet. The cold medicine begins to make me drowsy. Maybe if I just rest today I will kick this flu bug. I'll go in early tomorrow.

The phone by the bed wakes me like a fire alarm. They can't find the Johnson file. I hear the phones on the other end ringing in the background. I really should try to go in at noon. The report is due tomorrow.

I look in the closet for a warm sweater to wear. The skirt that matches it is in the ironing pile. I will press it after I sleep for a half hour. I turn up the dial on the electric blanket and crawl back into bed.

But I can't go to sleep. I pull myself back out of bed and make another cup of tea. There is one priority on my agenda for the day. It has to be done.

I turn on the answering machine.

Prayer

You know how much I'm needed at work, Lord, and how much my family needs me. Let me enjoy this chance to rest, but restore my health quickly. There's so much to do. In Jesus' name. Amen.

Gray Hair

Gray hair is a crown of splendor.
Proverbs 16:31

If gray hair is a crown of splendor, why does mine feel more like a crown of thorns? Why do I try to cover it with "light golden brown" dye? What am I really trying to hide? Could it be that I am getting old?

I'm not old! Sometimes I still feel like a young girl. I still love to teeter-totter. I love the circus. I love cotton candy. I feel a little wiser maybe, but certainly not old. If I really am "over the hill," then why do I feel like I'm still climbing?

I deserve every one of these silver hairs. Raising four children while trying to maintain a career has not been easy. But why can't this silver crown return to its original color for just a little while longer? I'm not quite ready for it.

I don't know why I'm so vain about my gray hairs. I accepted the laugh lines forming around my eyes. They remind me that I have had much to laugh about in this middle-aged life. I can even accept the middle-age spread. It means that I have lived abundantly. So why can't I accept this new salt-and-pepper style?

My husband has accepted his graying hair. I think he's glad to have hair. I tell him he looks distinguished.

When I complain about my gray, my husband tells me to look at his grandmother. She remarried at the age of 72 and just came back from a trip to Alaska. I don't think she's reached her peak, and she certainly isn't on the downhill side yet. Her steps may be a little slower, but she's still climbing. And she has the most beautiful silver hair that matches a sterling personality. Come to think of it, she loves the circus too.

Maybe on my next trip to the beauty parlor, I'll just have my hair frosted.

Prayer

Lord, help me accept with thanksgiving the life You've given me. My value is not in the quality of my life, the color of my hair, or the way I age. It comes from You. You have chosen me and made me Your child through Baptism. I don't need to fear getting older or to worry about my life. Christ has died and risen for me. Amen. Alleluia!

Doesn't Anyone Say Thank You Anymore?

Be joyful always; pray continually; give thanks in all circumstances, for this is God's will for you in Christ Jesus. *1 Thessalonians 5:16–18*

Sometimes, Lord, I get so frustrated. There are days when I don't seem to have a handle on anything: the kids, my job, the bills, the housework.

I don't think anyone really appreciates all I do. The kids nonchalantly walk across the just-mopped floor. The home I lovingly tried to put together is just a stopover, a place to grab a bite to eat and change into a clean shirt. Even my husband takes me for granted, leaving his dirty, wrong-side-out socks right next to the clothes hamper. My boss assumes the report will get done. And it does. He grabs it off my desk without so much as a simple thanks.

All I see at work and at home is more work. No one notices the fresh, clean clothes in the drawers. Instead, they want to know why their favorite shirt isn't clean. You know, the one they balled up and threw under the bed. And after I rush home to make a great meal, someone inevitably calls to tell me she won't be home for dinner. And my boss will always drop another project on my cluttered desk.

Why doesn't anyone ever say thank you any-more?

Why don't I?

Prayer

Jesus, help me do everything to Your glory, not request-ing or expecting thanks. Enable me to recognize and grate-fully accept the acts of kindness others offer to me. Thank You for taking my sins with You to the cross. Because of Your death, I have forgiveness for the times I am ungrate-ful. Thanks for the promise of new life I have through Your resurrection. Thanks for the gift of Your Spirit, who worked faith in my heart and strengthens me for all that I face. In Your name. Amen.

Comfort Me, Mom

[The Lord says,] "As a mother comforts her child, so will I comfort you." *Isaiah 66:13*

Lord, my mother can no longer comfort me, yet I still need her. I need the person she used to be. Strong, independent, resourceful.

Sometimes I want to feel her loving touch stroking back my stray hairs, even though some of them are now gray. I long for her loving attitude as she fixed my collar.

I especially need her sympathetic ear and a cup of spiced tea. I can almost feel her loving hand on my shoulder as I kneel beside the bed in prayer.

But now my mother needs me instead. She misplaces her glasses, forgets to pay the water bill, and gets confused over the Medicare brochure. She frantically calls in the middle of the night, crying that someone has stolen her watch.

"Did you look by the kitchen sink? Maybe you took it off when you did the dishes," I mutter in a sleepy drone.

"Oh, thank goodness, it's right here."

Now it's my privilege to stroke back the thinning gray hairs and take over buttoning her sweater when the gnarled hands fail. Now I can listen to her stories, even though I know them by heart.

I need to remember, though, that my mother still wants to be the young, vibrant person from my childhood. Aging is hard for her too.

I can never forget who the mother is. And I never want to forget the wonderful feelings and memories of being her child.

Prayer

Lord, forgive my impatience with my aging mother. Help me be as patient with her now as she was when she taught me how to crochet. Help me respect her advice and not see it as interference. Remind me that with age comes wisdom. Open my ears to listen, and give me an open mind and heart. Help me give Mom the support she needs. Make my steps slower to match hers as she once did for my baby steps. Give me a thankful spirit and a thankful attitude for this amazing woman. Let me always need her in the way only a daughter can need a mother. In Jesus' name. Amen.

The Ant

Go to the ant, you sluggard; consider its
ways and be wise! *Proverbs 6:6*

I'm exhausted tonight, Lord. But there are at least
two loads of laundry to do, and the supper dishes
cover the table. The kids are busy with homework.
Dare I ask them to help? No, homework is more
important.

But maybe they aren't really doing homework.
Maybe they are just hiding out, afraid I will ask them
to clean up the kitchen.

No, I better do it myself. If I can just pull myself
up off this couch, I'll feel better when it's all done. It's
just getting started. Well, maybe just a little nap first.
After all, I don't recall ever seeing an ant out after
dark.

Prayer

Energize me, Lord. Amen.

Chocolate Chip
Bran Muffins

But the temple He had spoken of was His
body. *John 2:21*

The latest diet book says that my body is my temple. So does the Bible. The diet book also says that fiber is the scrubber of my temple. Fiber is what cleans the cobwebs out of the corners and keeps these sometimes overworked parts running smooth. The book says bran is an excellent source of fiber and gives a recipe for bran muffins. But they are bland and boring. No sugar, no spice.

The most beautiful temple I've ever seen is St. John's Cathedral in New York. I don't remember how clean it was, but I do remember savoring the beauty of the stained-glass windows. Even in our little stone country church, a gentle beauty soothes me: flowers on the altar, much smaller stained-glass windows, colorful wall hangings the Sunday school kids made.

Now Lord, I know You want me to take care of this wonderful body that You have given me. I know I should keep it clean and help it run smoothly. But to this recipe for bran muffins, I will add just a few chocolate chips. I will savor the dark, sweet chocolate while getting the fiber.

Prayer

Thank You, dear Father, for fiber and for chocolate. A

well-balanced diet doesn't have to be boring. Help me take good care of my body, but help me be creative too! In Jesus' name. Amen.

Opening the Door

Love is patient. *1 Corinthians 13:4*

Already running late for work, I tried to coax the family cat out the door. "Come on, Barbie, don't you want out?"

She knew it was what I wanted, but she turned, flicked her long, furry tail in defiance, and jumped into my husband's recliner. She dared me to put down my lunch and briefcase to grab her. I had tried it yesterday, and she was anticipating the move. She crouched, ready to leap down the hallway and under the bed.

Barbra (she has a nose like Streisand, big blue eyes, and "sings" a lot) enjoys life on her terms. She relishes her freedom and lets nothing and no one get in her way. She attacks falling leaves with a vengeance and bravely walks across narrow picket fence tops.

Maybe that's why it feels so nice when she allows me into her life, when she brushes up against my leg as if to say, "You may pet me now." And no matter how busy or hurried I am, I take the time to pick her up and scratch under her chin.

I'm much more like my cat than I care to admit.

I'm independent and enjoy my freedom. I, like Barbie, can be elusive and defiant. The Lord in heaven wants me close to Him. He's even torn down all the barriers and made me His child. But I know better, and off I go on my own. I forget to pray or study His Word or receive His Sacrament. Only when my hectic, stressful lifestyle forces me into His arms do I remember He's always there for me. Always ready to pick me up and carry me.

Prayer

Dear Lord, thank You for allowing me the freedom to explore Your beautiful world. Thank You for bringing me into Your kingdom through my Baptism. Because of the faith You have given me, I know I can always turn to You for help and comfort. In Jesus' name. Amen.

Take a Hike, Jane Fonda!

He who ignores discipline despises himself. *Proverbs 15:32*

I really can't stand Jane Fonda. She's at least 15 years older than I am, yet she has the body of a 20-year-old.

I'd much rather not see her today. I feel exhausted and she is so ... so energetic. Her thighs are slim and her stomach is flat. When she prances around, nothing jiggles. And all those women on the tape with her are so cutesy. They have sleek, matching outfits right down to the socks. Even Jane's stepmother has a better body than mine! And here I am, in the same faded blue baggy sweats I wore yesterday. And green socks.

I feel frumpy.

But for some stupid reason—maybe punishment for the cheese Danish I wolfed down this morning—I reach for a tape anyway.

Let's see. We have *The Challenge* ... nah, too tired for that one. *Light Aerobics and Stress Reduction* ... no, I need more than that to burn off the Danish. *Complete Workout* ... no, too long. Ah yes, *Lower Body Solution*. Just right.

First, I have to rewind it. I got interrupted by a phone call last time and never finished it. I get the plastic step-up bench out of the closet. I bought it last year at a yard sale from a woman who goes to the Athletic Club. I didn't like her much either; she could pass for Jane's sister.

Warm up. Tap, tap. Biceps curls. Tap, tap. Heel, tap, walk.

I hate her music and wish she would use the oldies like Richard Simmons. I turn the volume on the TV down and plug the Beach Boys into the cassette player.

Up, down. Up, down. Do it again! I hate this step. It's complicated and I have to concentrate. Only 10 more minutes of aerobics. Tap, kick, and step. "One more time. Keep breathing!" Yeah, right. At least

Cindy Crawford lets me take a water break during her video.

Time for cool down? Already? I press *pause* on the VCR.

Whew. Now I'm ready to strengthen and tone. But again, I put in my own selection of music. *Sounds of His Love: The Forest.*

Birds chirp to "Come, Thou Fount of Every Blessing" as I do leg lifts.

I imagine myself beside a clear mountain stream as I work the outer hip and listen to "Be Still, My Soul."

I do sit-ups to "How Firm a Foundation." Appropriate.

Finally, we stretch, Jane and I. The sound of rushing water washes away the day's frustration, stress, and tension to the accompanying hymn, "Hiding in Thee."

I turn off the TV and lie flat on the floor, arms outstretched. I breathe deeply, shut my eyes, and listen to "Thou Art Worthy." The hymn is mixed with sounds of nature—birds, water, frogs.

The cassette tape ends with sounds of splashing water and I feel cleansed. Clean and strong.

Yeah, Jane. See you tomorrow.

Prayer

Gracious Father, thank You for the temple You have provided for me here on earth. Thank You for my hands, my feet, my head. Thank You for strong arms to wrap around my children. Thank You for strong legs so I can walk along the river and for eyes that see the astounding beauty of Your creation. Remind me always to treasure and care for it, even when it's the last thing I feel like doing. In Jesus' name. Amen.

Spring Cleaning

Do not store up for yourselves treasures on earth, where moth and rust destroy, and where thieves break in and steal. But store up for yourselves treasures in heaven, where moth and rust do not destroy, and where thieves do not break in and steal. For where your treasure is, there your heart will be also. *Matthew 6:19–21*

Is this really what I've worked so hard for all these years? All this stuff? I have more shoes than I will ever wear. I have clothes I haven't worn in more than a year. They hang, useless and dusty, in the back of my closet, which is crammed full of suits, silk blouses, T-shirts, and jogging outfits.

I need to do some serious spring cleaning, not only in my closet but in my mind as well. I need to weed out the useless and musty thought that I will ever wear short skirts again. I need to pack into boxes the idea that I need to be surrounded by material and pearl buttons for security. It is time to give away the notion that I need all this stuff, that someday I will wear the clogs and will use the leather purse that seemed so important to have at the time.

It is time to clean and simplify my way of thinking. I am not rich because of the lack of space in my cluttered closet. I am not poor because my power suits do not boast designer labels and the blouses are imitation silk.

Lord, wrench all this stuff out of my hands. Give me strength to be able to give my wool coat to someone who is cold. Give me wisdom to share this abundance and not hoard it away like a pack rat. As I clean this closet, help me dust away the idea that I will ever be a size five again. And as I release this thought, let me release my favorite dress and give it to the young single mother who needs it much more than I do. Help me learn to graciously give, not only the material things I have accumulated over the years, but the wisdom.

Prayer

Lord, as I clean this closet, help me throw out the misfit thoughts from the corners of my mind. Empower me to give generously as You have given to me. In Jesus' name. Amen.

Prairie Dog

Yet to all who received Him, to those who believed in His name, He gave the right to become children of God. *John 1:12*

God, sometimes I feel like a little prairie dog. I'm lost on the concrete freeway of Christian rhetoric and unable to dig a tunnel home.

As I listened to the speaker, I was confused by all the new Christian terms he shouted from the platform. Is this what religion is nowadays? Are we all dysfunctional cultists battling demons of inherited homosexual tendencies while combating new age and psychobabble? As I listened to the wise and learned orator, I felt like a small child among the Pharisees.

I wanted desperately to run for cover, but I did not know how to get off the freeway. I stood alone and afraid. I couldn't tunnel out of the situation.

Lord, where is the simple, dusty road of Christianity? Where is the simple, childlike faith that proclaims, "Jesus loves me, this I know"?

Thank You, Father, for guiding me home, back to my green pasture and still waters. Help me and all Christians hold onto the childlike faith that You gave us.

When we must venture beyond our pastures and cry out to the rest of the prairie dogs, keep our message true. Help us shout out not only the danger of the world but the glorious Good News of Your wonderful love shown when You sent Jesus as our Savior.

Please, Lord, don't let us lose the joy of knowing that we, like children, hold Your hand as You lead us across the busy, scary, confusing concrete freeway of life. Let us go forth and celebrate, proclaiming the angel's words, "Do not be afraid. I bring you good news of great joy that will be for all the people" (Luke 2:10).

Prayer

Thank You, heavenly Father, for the arrow in the shape of an old rugged cross that clearly marks the right road. In Jesus' name. Amen.

Lunch with the Girls

Even in laughter the heart may ache.
Proverbs 14:13

I didn't mean to be rude. I guess I should have known I would be bad company. I should have excused myself from lunch with the girls.

They were all so happy, laughing and telling jokes. I tried to join in, but my heart was breaking. And when Jeanne talked about the antics her son was pulling in college ... I never meant to be rude, but while her son was calling to describe college life, my daughter was calling to tell me she was pregnant.

I never expected my friends to understand, but maybe if I would have told them ... No, I couldn't. It would have spoiled everyone's lunch. So I simply smiled and pretended I was having a good time.

Why couldn't I tell them? Was I too proud? Or did I just want, for one hour, to pretend to myself that everything was fine? Did I want to keep my pain from them? Did I want to be a martyr and bear the burden alone?

I wonder how many times people have pretended with me. I would be hurt to know that others did not think my heart was big enough or understanding enough to listen to their pain.

Why is it so hard for me to let down my guard once in a while? Why do I feel I always have to be the strong one? Why do I find it so hard to cry in front of other people?

Why, Lord? Why do I think I have to smile all the time? Even when my heart has been slashed apart by one crisis or another? Do I think my lunch friends never cry? Am I foolish enough to think that I am the only one who is trying to keep my head above water in an angry sea of heartache?

Will I drown before I ever ask for a lifeline?

Prayer

Lord, help me share today's burden with a sister in Christ. Open my ears and heart to my friend's struggles as well. Help us encourage one another with Your promises of love and care. In Jesus' name. Amen.

A Time to Weep

Out of the depths I cry to You, O Lord.
Psalm 130:1

Sometimes a woman needs to cry.

There are times when a woman's emotions fill head and heart to the point of overflowing—a heated argument, the loss of a job, a prodigal child. Fear, passion, desperation, and stress push the arrow on the pressure gauge deep into the red zone and we begin to crack. And finally, we break down.

One small thing—a sad song, a cross word, a sentimental poem—pops the cork on our shaking bottle and tears spew forth the anger or sadness. Like a sudden summer shower, our emotions pelt down our cheeks and drip into clenched hands. Sometimes tears slowly drip like mist down leaded glass, gently cleansing away the dirt and dust and pain.

And perhaps the most wonderful part of the release valve is the dual purpose You created for tears. Not only are we sometimes overfilled with grief, but sometimes we are so filled with joy that we need a release from that emotion too.

The awe-inspiring beauties found on earth: a comforting hand, the birth of a child, an unexpected miracle, a race finally won. These fill us up, and tears are our release of the overabundant gladness.

Tears wash away pent-up feelings and bring a cleansing solace to the soul, a serenity. Hurts are gathered into a soggy tissue and thrown into the fire. Resentments that threatened are now worn on a shirt sleeve and quickly dry up.

Prayer

Thank You, gracious Father, for salty, streaming tears. Thank You for that welcome release valve in a woman's eyes; how brilliantly You formed us. How wise You were, even at the beginning of creation, when You gave women the ability to pour out some of the overflow in our souls.

Thank You for the many emotions that move a woman to tears. Thank You for so wisely giving us all the ability to cry. In Jesus' name. Amen.

Grant Me Patience, Now!

I wait for the Lord. *Psalm 130:5*

Lord, give me patience. And I need it now!

I have taken all I can. My faith in my job, my family, and myself is at an all-time low. I am still waiting to hear about my raise. I am still waiting to see if my husband will get the leaky faucet fixed. I am still waiting to hear my daughter say she has dropped the boyfriend who causes her, and the rest of the family, so much turmoil.

And I am waiting on You too, Lord. When are You going to answer my prayer for patience?

How I would love, right at this moment, to drive west into the warm, glowing sunset. To escape the constant waiting game. But here I am, going north and waiting for the light to turn green.

I wait in line at the store. The woman in front has a fistful of coupons, and my arm is cold and red from holding the pork chops and ice cream. She argues over the price of bananas, and we all wait for the man to run back and check the price. The woman behind me jams her cart into my legs and does not say excuse me. And I wait.

Road construction stops me on my way home. The ice cream melts while I wait, drumming my fingers on the steering wheel and wishing I had turned west.

I get home and the faucet is still dripping. My daughter is on the telephone with the focus of my prayers. My husband innocently asks me if I got my raise and I tell him no.

I check the mail ... bills, bills, bills. But wait! Here's the refund check from the IRS. I wondered when it would finally show up.

Prayer

Thanks, Lord. All things really do come in time. You answered my prayer for patience in many hidden ways today. You gave me the willpower not to say anything to the woman at the store. You gave me the wisdom to come home and not follow the impulse to drive away and forget the whole thing. You gave me patience to avoid angrily telling my daughter to hang up. And I just answered my husband instead of impatiently snapping back to his innocent question. And while my husband might someday fix the faucet, I think I'll just call the plumber for that. Thanks for my lesson in patience. In my Savior's name. Amen.

The Failure

"For I know the plans I have for you,"
declares the Lord, "plans to prosper you
and not to harm you, plans to give you
hope and a future." *Jeremiah 29:11*

God, why can't I shake this depression, this awful feeling of failure? It keeps churning around inside of me. I'm down so low that I can't see the way back up.

I tried my best, I know that. But it wasn't good enough. Now the fear of failing again has left me feeling weak, rejected, and vulnerable. I am terrified to try again.

I wanted to sail, but instead I failed. I wanted to fly, but instead I cried. My confidence has turned to impotence. Where did I go wrong, Lord? Did I expect too much? Was I too stupid, too smug, too unworthy to succeed?

And to add to this hurt, I am jealous of those who did achieve their goals. I should be happy for the ones who win instead of inwardly cursing their victory.

But I wanted to get the checkered flag. I wanted to bust through the tape at the end of the race. Now I am empty-handed, a loser.

This soft bed of self-pity I have made for myself feels pretty confining, but it is comforting. It would be easy to lie here and wallow in it. If I stay here, I'll never feel rejected again. If I don't try, I'll never have to worry about failing. All I have to do is lie here and make up some excuses. That should be pretty easy. I'm not tough enough, smart enough. I don't have what it takes. I wasn't blessed with the talent or the lucky breaks. Nice guys finish last.

Lord, I wanted it all to be perfect. Why didn't You make it that way?

I think I know why. Because when I hurt the worst, when I feel rejected and that I've failed, I turn to You. The hard shell that encased me suddenly shatters, and I am left with only the soft core of my soul. I have to admit I am not invincible, I am not perfect. And without that varnished exterior, I see and feel You more clearly. The pain awakens me to an understanding of the pain of others. I am forced to question my plans, my desires, my selfish wants and needs. And slowly the bed of self-pity becomes filled with rocks, irritating the softness of my soul.

Prayer

Lord, thank You for allowing me to fail at times. And thank You for Your strong hand that helps me out of this bed of self-pity, that gives me strength to keep getting up when I fall flat. In Jesus' name. Amen.

Hide-and-Seek

But seek first His kingdom and His righteousness, and all these things will be given to you as well. *Matthew 6:33*

Lord, where are You? I've looked for You everywhere this morning, but I can't seem to find You. Are You hiding from me? I've called Your name several times but don't seem to hear any answer. Have You turned a deaf ear to me? I searched for Your face among the crowd at church but did not see You anywhere. Were You there and I just failed to recognize You?

Lord, I think I know why You are avoiding me. I offended You, didn't I? I'm sorry. I never meant to neglect You this week. In fact, I missed our morning talks together and our quiet walks in the evening. I know it's a poor excuse, but I was terribly busy!

I forgot to block out time for You on my already crammed calendar. Somewhere among the high-lighted "important" trivialities of my daily life, I accidentally erased Your name. Instead of treating You like a special guest, I treated You like a Christmas card acquaintance—always meaning to call but never seeming to work it into my hectic schedule. And now that I'm ready to call, I am beginning to wonder if You've got an unlisted number.

I remember now that You left me a couple of messages during the week. One was attached to the peace rose beginning to bloom in the backyard. You beckoned me to stop, visit, and admire Your glorious handiwork, but I was late for a meeting and only gave You, and the rose, a passing glance. Then, You called out to me as You stood beside the woman stranded on the highway. But I didn't stop—I was on my lunch hour and pressed for time. All week, I returned none of Your messages.

Now that I have the afternoon off and am ready to spend some time with You, I suddenly know what it feels like to be kept waiting. Here I am, impatient as ever, wondering where You are. I guess You must have made other plans. And who could blame You, I haven't been a very good friend.

Prayer

Oh—there You are! I'm forgiven? Thank You, wonderful Lord. You are always there waiting with open arms. Help me spend more time with You from now on. Help me make You my number one priority. I have really missed You! Let's go out to the garden and visit; there is so much I want to tell You. And I really want to see that rose. It's probably in full bloom by now, and if I don't see it today, tomorrow it may be gone. In Jesus' name. Amen.

Falling Together

He is before all things, and in Him all
things hold together. *Colossians 1:17*

Thank You, God, for saving my life.

Just when I thought I'd hit bottom, another crisis pushed me over the edge. I thought I'd lost You, God, that You had given up and released the rope. When my life was falling apart, I prayed that You would catch me.

I kept falling.

But I never hit bottom.

I fell smack into Your open hands. It wasn't You who let go of the rope, it was me. I was too weak to hold on. The fall left me battered and bruised, but nothing is broken and I will heal. I am stronger and wiser now, a more experienced climber. Now I know which ropes are a stronghold and which ropes will carry little weight.

You never gave up, never left me stranded on the dangerous, rocky ledge. You knew I would eventually tumble. You knew I would eventually have to let go. And only when I let go of the weak, earthly ropes I was clinging to, could You make the pieces of my life fall together.

Prayer

Thank You, Lord, for catching me when I fall apart, when I am at the end of my rope and too weak to hang on. You have promised always to be there for me. You even sent Your Son, Jesus, to suffer and die to win my release from Satan's hold. Then You raised Him from the dead so that I need never fear this world or death. You have "taught me the ropes" by giving me Your Spirit to work faith in my heart. And this faith binds me tightly to You. In Jesus' name. Amen.

Charge It

[Jesus said,] "No one can serve two masters. ...
You cannot serve both God and Money."
Matthew 6:24

I am in deep, deep trouble. Bills overflow the mailbox, but there's no money in the bank.

It was so easy. The credit cards came without even applying for them. And now it's time to pay up. Easy money carries tough consequences.

I pulled out the cards for what I thought were needs. The purchases turned out to be frivolous wants. Even though most of what I charged was on sale, paying in hard-earned cash would have decreased the amount I bought.

I didn't realize the mess I could create just by signing my name on a little piece of paper. I'm still paying for the great Christmas presents I gave everyone, and it's July. At least on Independence Day I paid off one card. What freedom!

I hereby declare my independence from credit cards. I will take my scissors and cut up these binding, plastic chains. From now on, I am in "charge."

Prayer

Lord, the worst thing about being in debt is the feeling of being mastered by money, not You. Guard me against the temptation of "easy payment plans." Remind me how difficult it is to put You first when money blinds my every turn. Forgive me for Jesus' sake for my financial indiscre-

tions. Strengthen me to make wiser choices with the financial gifts You provide for me. In Jesus' name. Amen.

The Fire

For where your treasure is, there your
heart will be also. *Matthew 6:21*

The bird was stiff in his metal cage, but the toilet paper remained untouched on the roll.

The pink sweater was scorched and soggy, but the dust under the bed was still there.

The bottle of ketchup in the refrigerator was a crimson glob of goo, but the pig trivet peeked out from beneath the ashes.

The picture frames were blackened with soot, but the faces underneath gleamed with smiles.

Broken glass was scattered in the flower beds, but the columbines bloomed anyway.

People came from miles around to view the destruction and to offer helping hands.

The old heirlooms are gone forever, but the memories remain intact.

The welcome mat is still at the door.

Prayer

Lord, I weep over the fire's destruction, the blackened walls, the soggy, soot-filled carpets, the treasures that have been destroyed. Yet I will give thanks. My family is still intact. We are all still alive, both in body and spirit. Thank You, God. Thank You. Instead of concentrating on building up earthly treasure, focus my eyes on You—the treasure that cannot be destroyed. In Jesus' name. Amen.

I Am Not a Quitter!

Delight yourself in the Lord and He will give you the desires of your heart. *Psalm 37:4*

Lord, is this really what You wanted me to do? When I prayed about taking on this challenge, I thought You were behind me. I never thought it would be so hard. I didn't know it would demand so much.

You gave me the talent. Help me keep at it.

You gave me the ability. Also give me the determination.

You blessed me with the idea. Enable me to persevere and see it through.

You gave me the Light. Lead me steadily towards it.

You set me on the path. Guide me along it.

You gave me the challenge. Give me willingness to make the necessary sacrifices.

Prayer

God, You have given so much already, and I thank You for it. Please, as I struggle to make this dream a reality, give me the strength not to procrastinate when the going gets tough and the tenacity to declare that I am not a quitter! Jesus asked You in the garden if Your will was still for Him to suffer and die. I guess I'm asking You to reconfirm Your plan for me. Not as I will, but as You will. I trust my life to You. In Jesus' name. Amen.

The Dinner Party

"Martha, Martha," the Lord answered, "you are worried and upset about many things, but only one thing is needed." *Luke 10:41–42*

I wanted everything to be perfect for my dinner guests. I cleaned house for two days and tried to make dishes that stretched my cooking capabilities. I diligently refreshed drinks and kept pillows on the couch straightened. I wanted desperately to impress everyone.

But they weren't. I didn't listen as the woman talked about her children. I was busy in the kitchen. I failed to acknowledge the cheesecake another guest graciously brought for dessert. I was hastily clearing away the dinner dishes.

The table may have been stunning, but everyone felt uncomfortable. No one felt at home because I treated them like ... like guests, not like friends or family.

I forgot the most important ingredient at my dinner party. I forgot to ask for Your presence here, Lord. I forgot to sit down and visit with my friends as Mary did with You. I was too busy playing Martha.

Prayer

Lord, the one thing I need is Your presence in my life. When things gets out of balance, pull me up and set me straight. I can't entertain others unless I'm a participant in the event. It's like learning from You. It doesn't come by osmosis. Make me more like Mary, listening to Your every word. Through Bible study and worship, reveal the things of real importance—Your suffering, death, and resurrection that won me life forever. Then when I'm around my friends, make me a witness of this wonderful, impressive gift. In Your name. Amen.

Die ... it!

The cheerful heart has a continual feast.
Proverbs 15:15

First, there was the retirement dinner on Friday. That small piece of cheesecake seemed the perfect reward for losing two pounds. Then on Saturday there was a birthday party. What's chocolate cake without ice cream? And on Sunday I couldn't offend my mother-in-law by turning down a second helping of her famous lasagna.

Because I ate so much over the weekend—

again—I managed to gain back the two pounds I lost last week, plus a couple more.

A walk would have been great, but when did I have time? I ran the vacuum, doesn't that count for something? I could have done sit-ups while watching the football game, but the couch seemed lonely for company.

Now I will have to start all over again. On Monday I will be faithful—diet shakes and a salad. On Tuesday I won't put butter on the broccoli. I'll sneak only one cookie after dinner on Wednesday. While the smell of buttered popcorn on Thursday will make my mouth water, I'll eat mine dry. On Friday I'll eat only one piece of pizza. But Saturday? Let's see, that's Erin's wedding and ...

Prayer

Lord, it would be so easy to diet if there were no reason to celebrate. Even at work there always seems to be goodies for one reason or another: the birth of a baby, a promotion, even donuts from the football pool winner. Help me remember there will be no celebration if I don't lose some weight. I can't think of a bigger reason to cheer than achieving my goal of losing a few pounds. Yes, laughter and lasagna seem to go together, but help me learn to laugh without it. I want to be a good steward of the body You have given me. In Jesus' name. Amen.

An Imperfect Christian

Mary Magdalene went to the disciples
with the news: "I have seen the Lord!"
John 20:18

Sometimes I feel so inadequate. I say things I shouldn't. I feel things that a Christian woman shouldn't feel. I want desperately to be Your faithful follower, Lord, and so many times I fall short.

There are days I get angry and feel like screaming. Sometimes I do. I want to be honest, caring, and happy, but sometimes the feelings just aren't there. I get cross with those I love, even cross at You.

Sometimes I bargain with You just to get my own selfish way. I want You to use me for Your good purpose, just as long as it doesn't cause me any inconvenience.

Sometimes I feel a little better than someone else, and sometimes I feel I don't measure up to a snail on the sidewalk. I lose my perspective and my purpose here on earth. In times of discouragement, I lose my trust and faith in You. I forget the many wonderful blessings in my life and see only the dirt and grime.

Prayer

Lord, forgive me. Thank You for my brain. Forgive me when it works a little overtime in the "feel sorry for myself" mode. Thank You for my heart that keeps on beating even when I have a bad day. And thank You for the soul that knows that You forgive my shortcomings, my inadequacies that remind me I am flesh and bone—a sinner. Remind me that among the first people You spoke to after Your resurrection was a former prostitute, Mary Magdalene. You came to be perfect for us because we never will be perfect. Only in You is my weakness turned to strength. Create in me a new spirit, one that trusts You for my self-worth. A spirit that focuses on You, the Author and Perfecter of my faith. In Your name. Amen.

The Cat in the Hat

My times are in Your hands. *Psalm 31:15*

I feel like the cat in the hat in my son's Dr. Seuss book. I am holding a cup and a cake, two books and a fish, a little toy ship, some milk and a dish. I hop around from one foot to the other, trying not to drop or break anything. I frantically try to balance everything in my hectic life.

Yet here I am, reaching out for another challenge. I really want to sign up for that college class, but can I juggle yet another thing in these already overloaded hands? I need to put down something before I pick up something else.

Maybe I could drop my exercise class and walk during my lunch hour. But then I would have to give up the enjoyable lunches I have with friends.

I could pass on my weekly writing group, but it's the inspiration that keeps me going when rejection slips come too quickly.

I could say no to the bowling league, but that's mother-daughter time, even if we do throw more than our fair share of gutter balls.

I could drop evening story time with my son, but then I would never know if the pioneer family made it to Oregon.

Maybe if I wiggle a little to the right and perch the class on top between the cake and the dish …

Prayer

Lord, how do I juggle all I want to do? I only have two hands, but everything I am holding seems like a treasure. Give me insight to the things You want me to do. Let me always look to You for guidance to make the right choices. If it's part of Your plan for me, You will provide the way to "balance" my life. In Jesus' name. Amen.

Bless Me with Wings

Oh, that I had the wings of a dove! I would fly away and be at rest—I would flee far away and stay in the desert; I would hurry to my place of shelter, far from the tempest and storm. *Psalm 55:6–8*

Where can I go to escape? I wish I had a cabin somewhere deep in the mountains. A place with no phones, no children ... and no worries.

Weariness pulls me down. I can't get up and face another day. I cry for help but no one comes. Confusion and chaos surround me.

My workplace is unorganized. Everyone is overworked and underpaid. No one can offer a helping hand because we are all operating at the maximum. Our stress has reached the boiling point.

Then I go home where discontent and disorder reign. There's no toilet paper in the bathroom. I just can't face the supper dishes. And laundry reaches to the ceiling.

Please, God, give me strength. Help me face my tasks. Put a smile on my face and in my weary heart.

Bless my house. Let the beauty shine amid the clutter. Lighten my attitude so the task will be joyful.

Bless my job. Bring organization to my desk ... and my thoughts. Remind me to compliment and compromise. Don't let the annoying distractions prevent me from doing my job to Your glory.

And finally, Lord, bless me with wings. Provide a release for the stress that leaves me weak and tired. Help me speak to my boss about extra help and delegate household chores.

Give me strength until next weekend. Then I will make reservations at that cozy cabin in the mountains. A time to retreat and regroup—just You, me, and a good book.

Prayer

Carry me on Your wings, Almighty Lord. Let Your healing love wash over me and restore me. Then gently set me down to continue working for You. In Jesus' name. Amen.

The Reunion

The race is not to the swift or the battle to
the strong, nor does food come to the wise
or wealth to the brilliant or favor to the
learned; but time and chance happen to
them all. *Ecclesiastes 9:11*

Thank You, Lord, for the wonderful time at my class reunion. Despite the nervous vanity that accused me of no longer looking like a slim cheerleader, I had a great time renewing old acquaintances.

But something else kept nagging me on the way to the reunion. The question played in my head like a stuck record: After 20 years, am I a success? What would my classmates think? I don't have a fancy house or a Mercedes parked in the garage. There's still no college degree on my wall, and I am a long way from becoming the president of anything.

But among friends, I discovered the real meaning of success. As we reminisced in the warm sunshine, I felt a wonderful sense of gratitude for my childhood and for the classmates who are still friends. We share a special bond, even 20 years later.

Success is not a pinnacle to be reached after 20 years in the real world. It isn't money in the bank or being the CEO of a corporation. Success is a lifelong road that we still travel. Sometimes we think we've reached the end of the road, only to find it is just another fork.

Success is being a single parent and earning your college degree while working two jobs. Success is fulfilling a long-held dream to train horses while still struggling to have the child you desperately long to hold in your arms. Success is going back to school after being laid off from a job you've held for 15 years.

Prayer

Dear Lord, I know success really depends on You. I see that so much more clearly now. You are working in all of us—whether we've been in church for the past 20 years or only recently been made Your child. I see Your presence in the life of all my former classmates. You have chosen us, saved us, and given us tasks to do in Your kingdom. Be with us as we complete our individual roads to the ultimate success—life with You in heaven. In Jesus' saving name. Amen.

Working Late

For we are God's fellow workers; you are God's field, God's building. *1 Corinthians 3:9*

Why tonight, of all nights, did I decide to work late? I really needed to catch up on paperwork. An hour of no interruptions, no phones, no customers.

But just as I began digging into the pile, a co-worker stopped by to say goodnight. As she began telling me about a problem she had been having at home, I thought, I don't have time for this. Forty-five minutes later, she finally left.

The filing didn't get done. My best-laid plans had gone awry. But You knew they would, didn't You, God?

My co-worker needed a friend, a shoulder to cry on. Thank You, God, for making me available. Paperwork isn't a top priority in my job or in my life. People are. Thank You for giving me an open ear and a strong shoulder. Thank You for reminding me that an open door for co-workers is always better than a cold shoulder.

Thank You for the hour that I worked late because tonight I wasn't working for the bank, I was working for You.

Prayer

Lord, sometimes I shut out the whispered pleas for help. Let someone else do it, I grumble, I'm busy. But You're never too busy for me. You invite me to bring anything to You at anytime. You pick me up, listen to me, comfort me, and guide me to the right choices. One choice You guided me to was listening to my co-worker. Thank You for putting me in the right place at the right time. Be with her as she deals with the problem. Give me the ability to support her during this difficult time. Thank You, Lord, for always being here. In Jesus' name. Amen.

The Healing Touch

He heals the brokenhearted and binds up
their wounds. *Psalm 147:3*

My daughter flew down the track, her chestnut
ponytail flying in the breeze. She was in the lead with
only one more hurdle to go. The tape was in sight.

Then it happened. Her back foot didn't quite
clear the last hurdle, and she fell flat. Her hands and
knees skidded on the rough pavement, and cinders
dug into her soft skin.

"I was so close, Mom," she cried, limping painful-
ly to the locker room. The coach handed me a tweez-
ers and a bottle of antiseptic. As I carefully washed
away the debris, the cleansing hurt worse than the
fall. It hurt worse than losing the race. I applied a
soothing salve and bandaged her wounds in soft
white gauze.

Prayer

*Dearest Father, You understand the agony a parent
feels. You cheer me on, only to watch me fall flat. Then You
pick me up and cleanse my raw wounds as I wince in
agony. You feel my pain. You reassure me that I will heal
and that I will finish the race and win. Your Son has
already gone through the most painful cleansing for me. I
am Your child because of His sacrifice on the cross. When
I fail, I call on His name for forgiveness and I hold out my
soul to You so You can wash away the sin. Then You
restore my spirit with soothing words of promise and inspir-
ing words of hope. In my Savior's name I pray. Amen.*

A Little Soap and Water

When [Jesus] had finished washing their feet, He put on His clothes and returned to His place. "Do you understand what I have done for you?" He asked them. *John 13:12*

Shorty is an old cowboy who stands about five feet tall. He always dresses in clean blue jeans and western shirts with pearl snaps. He is never seen without his silver-bellied Stetson hat and his "girlfriend," a bottle of portable oxygen. "She's always by my side and never talks back unless I knock her over," he quips. "Then she squeals like a cat with its tail in the wringer!" Shorty is never without a smile and a good story to tell. The weathered old man is high on my list of favorite customers.

I hadn't seen Shorty for quite a while. He finally came into the bank, looking pale and haggard. He said he was feeling like "a horse that had been rode hard and put away wet."

"Where have you been, Shorty?" I asked.

"I been up to the hospital," he replied.

As he told me about his stay in the hospital, a flicker of a tear came into the old man's kind blue eyes. "Now I'm used to being a pretty independent sort. Always been able to take care of myself."

It is something Shorty does well. He is fastidious about his looks. Even the old Stetson was well cared for.

"I've never been one to ask for help, but after laying in that bed for a couple of days, I was feeling pretty grimy. I'm used to a good scrubbing every day. I asked the nurse for a basin of water and a bar of soap, but she was in a hurry. Said she would bring it later."

It was hard to imagine the old cowboy in a stark white hospital bed wearing one of those open-backed gowns.

"By afternoon, she still hadn't come back with the water, so I buzzed that red button by my bed. The nurse came a runnin'. I asked her again for some water and a little soap. She grumbled and gave me an impatient glare. You know, that took away what little bit was left of my dignity. I pleaded with her, telling her all I wanted to do was wash my hands."

Shorty held his gnarled old hands out to me, his eyes begging for understanding.

"I guess that's about the worst part of gettin' old. It's bad enough having to ask for help, but it's losing my pride that gets me the most. All I wanted to do was wash my hands."

Prayer

Lord, the next time I am impatient with an elderly person, or worse yet, I talk down to them like a small child, help me remember Shorty's outstretched hands. Teach me to gracefully assist others without stripping them of their dignity. Let me serve others as unselfishly as You serve me. In Your name. Amen.

Fired Up

Do your best to present yourself to God as
one approved, a workman who does not
need to be ashamed and who correctly
handles the word of truth. *2 Timothy 2:15*

Roberta was lovingly referred to at the bank as
"The Mom." She was constantly cleaning out her
freezer and bringing delicious goodies. Her cinnamon
rolls were as big as a dinner plate. If an ache or pain
was mentioned, she advised a remedy. If someone
complained about the weather, she had a positive
comeback. "All this rain has the fields looking so
green!"

But with all her wonderful qualities, Roberta had
a major fault. She could not balance her accounts at
the end of the day. She gave it her best, but that was
not good enough and she was fired.

There wasn't a farewell party. After all the goodies
she supplied for the birthday parties and baby show-
ers, no one baked for her. But we missed her deeply.

I read an article about how women over 50 have
a real struggle trying to find a job. I worried about
Roberta. I should have known better.

The other day I met her for lunch and asked her
how things were going. "I made Virginia a lemon pie yesterday," she said. "She's been laid up with a broken hip."

Roberta is busy baking, sewing, and painting.
She's reading a 100-year-old book that belongs to her
grandmother.

"Now I have the time to get to some of the things I never had time to do before," she added. "I even took one of the bugs that was eating at my roses and put it under a microscope."

The waitress brought our iced tea and Roberta grabbed my hands. "Let's pray," she said.

"Dear Father, thank You so much for this glorious day. Thank You for this chance to be together." Her voice glowed with warmth and enthusiasm.

As we spoke of her dismissal from the bank, I told Roberta how sorry we all were.

Roberta, in that wise and motherly voice I had often admired, replied, "It was hard. I had a lot of bad feelings at first. I was embarrassed and ashamed. I doubted myself and was terribly hurt. But I know the Lord is watching over me. He simply has other plans for my life."

Then she mentioned that she is thinking of taking a nursing course at the vocational school. "But I will go wherever the Lord chooses to send me," she firmly added.

Prayer

Gracious and wise Father, being fired is never easy. It hurts. But what a comfort to know Roberta's right. You did have a plan for her life. Yesterday she told me all about her new job at the doctor's office. Thank You for watching over all of us and moving us in the direction that You want us to take. In Jesus' name. Amen.

Get It in Gear!

Why are you downcast, O my soul? Why
so disturbed within me? *Psalm 43:5*

What am I so impatient about? I have been
blessed with so much in my life: a good job, a warm
home, a caring husband, four healthy kids. But I want
more. This restlessness consumes my life.

There's so much yet to learn, so much I haven't
tried. I want to play the piano, swim in the ocean, and
have tea in the famous Vancouver castle. More than
anything, I want to go back to college. Instead, I'm
ironing a dress for work tomorrow.

I feel like life is passing me by—quickly. Day by
day, week by week, month by month, I dream of all
the things I have not done, books I have not read,
places I have not seen.

When I took night classes a couple of years ago, I
felt guilty for leaving my family to fend for themselves. When I attended a three-day seminar, I felt
guilty for not being there when my son got the flu
and my husband had to take off work. Frankly, I got
tired of lugging around the heavy burden of guilt, so I
set it aside, along with my dream.

Is it possible, God, to pursue my own dreams and
still be a responsible parent and wife? Is it wrong to
have goals, knowing that I will not always be there for
the people I love the most?

I tell my children that they can be anything they
want to be in this life. But the words seem hollow and

empty. It must look like I simply gave up, I quit when the going got tough.

When I took a literature class, I was able to share a wonderful poem with my daughter. The words of Robert Frost still echo in my mind. Am I willing to take the road "less traveled by"?

Prayer

Thank You, God, for helping me realize that this muddy rut I am in is of my own making. My spinning wheels bogged me down even further. My kids will survive, even if I'm not there every moment. If I share what I learn, we'll all be better off. If I show them that I can be everything I want to be—they will see that they can too. And when I finally have that diploma in my hands, we'll all know that goals can be achieved. Guide me, God. Give me the strength to make this dream a reality. I know nothing is impossible with You by my side. College, here I come! In Jesus' name. Amen.

SECTION 6

LIFE SAVORS

Penguins and Platypuses

A cheerful heart is good medicine. *Proverbs 17:22*

Judy, my trusted friend and co-worker, made me laugh at work. It wasn't just an ordinary, everyday snicker or titter but a real thigh-slapping belly laugh, the kind that bursts forth uncontrollably like a colorful, glorious bloom.

The more Judy and I tried to control our sudden outburst, the funnier everything became. We giggled at the broken copy machine and suddenly, her skirt belt broke. We roared!

Customers smiled and shook their heads. A few laughed along with us, even though they didn't know what had tickled us so. Tears streamed down our cheeks, and my sides ached with the kind of pain that reawakens a mundane day. Our laughter was as cleansing and refreshing as a sudden summer shower.

Almighty Creator, I think when You look down at this crazy, zany world, You must let out a good long guffaw once in a while too. Your wonderful, witty sense of humor abounds. I grin when I see a platypus, and I chuckle at penguins. Donkeys are a riot! The antics of the monkeys at the zoo never fail to turn a gloom-and-doom day into a comical celebration.

Prayer

Thank You, Lord, for helping this staunch, career-minded superwoman remember that life isn't meant to be taken so seriously. Thank You for creating penguins and platypuses. Thank You for creating people like Judy, who bring a black-and-white world the gift of colorful, contagious, blooming laughter. In Your saving name. Amen.

A Voice in the Stillness

Be still, and know that I am God. *Psalm 46:10*

Early on a Saturday morning, my 7-year-old is still snuggled under his Mickey Mouse comforter. The sleepy sun has yet to peek over the horizon.

I sit with a cup of coffee in my favorite chair, an afghan tucked around me. For the first time this week, I have a moment to myself.

I want to pray; somehow during the last five hectic days, I could never find the time. But the words won't come. My mind, like my home, is quiet.

Instead, I look out the frosted windowpanes. The dog sleeps contentedly in his house. The tree branches, covered with ice and the falling snow, twinkle like thousands of tiny crystals as the light of the sinking moon passes through them. A serene white stillness blankets the earth.

I begin again to talk to my Father.

Prayer

I realize, Lord, that it's not only the first time this week that I've taken time to pray, it's the first time I've slowed down long enough to listen. Your answer is the sound of stillness. And Your message comes through loud and clear. In Jesus' name I pray. Amen.

The Bread of Human Kindness

I led them with cords of human kindness,
with ties of love; I lifted the yoke from
their neck and bent down to feed them.
Hosea 11:4

It was one of *those* Mondays. The day had started with a broken bottle of maple syrup, and it was only getting stickier.

I hurried into the copy room to make a duplicate of a customer's statement. The machine jammed. Then the red light flashed, which indicates it needs toner. My stomach growled, reminding me that a few quick bites of a dry pancake does not qualify as a nutritious or satisfying breakfast.

I returned to my desk only to be greeted by yet another customer. Smiling on the outside, I said hello, but my inner voice grumbled at this interruption.

The man handed me a foil-wrapped package. "The wife bought too many bananas last week. They were on sale, and you know how she is about sales," he explained. "She whipped up a batch of banana bread and thought you might like a loaf."

I didn't know what to say. He was not a friend, not even a regular customer. I had only met his wife once, and no, I don't know how she is about food sales. "Thanks," I managed to mutter, taken aback at the couple's surprise act of kindness.

"No thanks necessary. I'm just glad I won't be eating banana bread for the next month." He grinned and was gone.

I poured my full cup of cold coffee down the drain and started a fresh pot. The banana bread was warm, sweet, and moist. As I headed back to my desk with a fresh attitude, angry words spewed from the copy room. "This stupid machine! Instead of an 'out of order' sign, it needs to have a red light indicating when it actually works!"

I unwrapped my foil package of kindness and shared.

Prayer

Lord, thank You for small acts of kindness that lighten the load … and for reminding me that it's nice to share. In Jesus' name. Amen.

The Fountain Pen

Sing praises to God, sing praises. *Psalm 47:6*

I found my fountain pen! Thanks, Lord! My son borrowed it and forgot to return it. He likes the way it writes, the feel of it between his fingers. He can write larger and clearer with my pen. I know what I'm getting him for his birthday.

It feels great to have my fountain pen back. Heavy and larger than other writing instruments, it's elegantly styled with black and gold stripes. When I put the finely honed tip to paper, I feel like I'm writing something important. I could be signing a bill into law or scrolling my name on the Declaration of Independence.

I used the fountain pen to record my grandson Daniel's birth in the family Bible. And my fountain pen flows across my journal as I write. This private declaration of independence records my thought. Just putting the jumbled ideas and worries onto paper brings a sense of freedom.

As I write out my worries, my dreams, my heartaches, my joy, and even my depressing self-doubt, these fountain-pen thoughts take up a page in the book of my life. A page I can turn. And there before me is a new page, blank except for the fine straight lines waiting to be filled.

Prayer

Lord, as I reread the lined tablets of my life, I see the

many blessings You have poured out on me. I see a gush-ing fountain of understanding and pools of grace. I see the most precious gift of Your Son, my Savior. I see the faith You have instilled in my heart. When I grow old and my eyes begin to fail, when the words I have written become faded on the yellowed pages, help me see more clearly what has been recorded. Hold before me the answered prayers and the miracles that occurred, even though I was too blind to see. Help me read again Your promises of comfort and hope that have come true. Send Your Spirit to help me raise my voice as I sing Your prais-es. In Jesus' name. Amen.

Coasting

Every valley shall be filled in, every moun-tain and hill made low. The crooked roads shall become straight, the rough ways smooth. *Luke 3:5*

Thank You, Lord, for this coasting time. I sit in a clean house. No mountains of laundry wait to be done. Fresh-smelling towels are tucked in the bath-room cabinet. Even the socks (most of them anyway) have mates and snuggle in dresser drawers.

Grandma has the kids for the night, and a serene quietness pervades the house. Even my husband is away fishing. I have no deadlines and no dinner par-ties—just cheese and crackers for dinner and yogurt for dessert. It's a flat road under a blue sky—what a day!

Prayer

What a peaceful, wonderful day You have created, Lord. It's nice to be able to sit in a quiet house and talk with You. And to top it all off, I have all the housework done and nothing for the rest of the weekend—and I have Monday off! Thanks, Lord, for the break. During this "coasting" time, renew my spirit. Feed my soul on Your Word and remind me of Your promises. In Jesus' name I ask this. Amen.

Old Things

Rise in the presence of the aged, show respect for the elderly and revere your God. I am the Lord. *Leviticus 19:32*

It seems the older I get, the more beauty I find in old things: delicate yellowed lace, weathered old barns, antique clocks that dependably chime out the quarter hours.

I'm just beginning to appreciate the idea that old things hold unique qualities. Just look at the spark of imagination in toys that don't require batteries. Or the skill, patience, and pride that goes into handcrafted furniture. Some perfume bottles are tiny, intricate works of art meant to be treasured long after the liquid is gone. And baby dolls with porcelain faces must be treated as gently as the real thing.

There is a special loveliness in timeworn things. Strength in aged trees standing proud as a fortress. Dignity in fine vintage kid gloves. Peacefulness in ticking mantle clocks. Fragility in rose-covered china teacups.

Old things develop character from years of use. Each nick and scratch tells a story. The condition of the antique talks volumes about the family it served. Maybe that's why I'm developing an appreciation of old things. I'd like to think that over the years, God has developed me into a unique character.

God's used the weather of sadness and joy to polish me and shape me into His creation. The nicks and scratches of hard times have toughened me and brought me to a reliance on my heavenly Father. Through the years, God has made me His child, crafted me into His follower, and kept me safe in His arms. Like a battered antique, I am precious to my owner—God.

Prayer

Dear Lord, thank You for the years of life that You have given me. Thank You for helping me realize the value of "old" things. Keep me from sagging under the thought of aging. Instead give me the strength of the oak tree, the pliable personality of worn leather, and a flavorful spirit like vintage wine. Instill in me appreciation for old-fashioned values and help me adapt to new ideas that don't conflict with Your Word. Thank You for bringing me through the "weather" of life and keeping me safe as Your treasured child. In Jesus' name. Amen.

Love Letters

Encourage each other. *1 Thessalonians 4:18*

It came on the day I was frustrated from trying to organize our income taxes. The card's illustration showed a bunch of gray hares lying on a bathroom floor. My friend had sent me a bit of sunshine in the card, unaware it would arrive on a day when I needed a good laugh. The card sat on my desk for more than a month before I put it away in my "Special" file, which contains all the bits of sunshine acquired through my mailbox.

Every day I anxiously await the mailman. I know the sound of his truck and worry if he's late. Each day, opening the silver box is like opening a surprise package.

It started when I was a child. My grandmother sent me weekly letters. Tucked into each envelope was something special—a children's crossword puzzle cut from the newspaper, a funny poem, or a pressed flower.

In high school, I stopped at the post office after school, anxious for a letter from a boyfriend away at college. I have long since lost touch with him, but the memory of hiding his love letters deep in a pocket until I could read them alone still lingers. The words were secret and sweet.

As birthdays came, I saved all the special cards, some sentimental, some silly. I saved the sympathy cards delivered after my husband died. Each one gave me a unique message of hope and made me realize that I was not as alone as I felt.

I look through my "Special" file when I feel gray and gloomy. I touch the handmade Christmas card from an elderly gentleman. I smile at the thank-you card from a customer. I wipe away a tear as I reread a card from my daughter at college that says "Thanks, Mom, for everything and for putting up with me!" I look at the pictures sent from far away of nieces and nephews I see very rarely. I treasure a boss' memo that says the job was well done.

Many think letter writing is a waste of time. And sometimes, with my busy life, I feel that way too. But on a recent visit to my mother, I noticed that she carried a letter I had written a month earlier in her purse. The envelope was worn, as if its contents had been taken out and read many times. She pulled out the pictures I had sent and showed them off to a friend at the grocery store. Only then did I realize the gift of love she had received from the hastily composed note and pictures of the grandkids.

Prayer

Thank You, Father, for all the love I have received from the bright silver box at the end of the lane. Thank You for the letters in Your book that have brought me strength, wisdom, inspiration, and a constant reminder of Your love for me. Guide me as I send my own bits of sunshine to those who have lightened my day. Let me be a light upon the hill through my words and actions and letters. In Jesus' name. Amen.

Angel Windows

And God saw that it was good. *Genesis 1:25*

I wonder if angels have the same view of earth that I have from an airplane. Do they look down on wispy, cottonball clouds, patchwork-quilt fields, and neat rows of homes with tiny squares of green? From up here, the aspens paint the mountains in splendor as they turn from green to gold and the oak brush scatters in splashes of crimson. Even the interesting formations of the adobe hills create a strange beauty.

From high above, the paths of streams and rivers and the dots of small lakes and ponds indicate well-reasoned planning for the nourishment of the land. Everything ties together with finite precision. From the skies, it's so apparent how well designed this universe is.

Seasoned fliers read their papers and scribble in crossword puzzle books. They cluck their tongues when they see me gazing out the tiny window like a child. Yep, amateur flier, they must think. I want to tug on their sleeves and cry out in amazement, "See that?"

How incredible it would be to have my own set of wings—to be able to skim the treetops and soar at sunset over a clear mountain lake. I could feel the wind in my hair as I trace from the air the intricate landscapes God so intelligently designed.

Prayer

Almighty Creator, as I look out the window of the plane, it is all so very, very good. Thank You. In Your Son's name. Amen.

The Tattered Old Bible

Your word is truth. *John 17:17*

Frayed on the edges, some of the yellowed pages are even torn from the string binding. The tattered leather cover, once as shiny and stiff as a new shoe, now falls limp, its edges curling toward the pages.

It was my grandmother's Bible and her mother's before her. Faded handwriting fills the margins, much of it now illegible. But on the back cover, I can still make out a few words: "They will soar on wings like eagles ..."

My grandmother handed me this Bible when I was a small child. I had taken a jar of old coins to the attic for my "store" and had forgotten to return them to her desk. She asked me if I took the coins, but I meekly told her no. I was afraid to tell the truth.

Grandmother gave me an odd look but said nothing. All night, I tossed and turned as voices in my head cried out, "Liar, liar! Pants on fire!" Why, why couldn't I tell her the truth?

The next morning I awoke to the sound of pipes rattling as Grandma filled the teakettle. I sheepishly crept into the kitchen. Grandma sat at the table with the old Bible. She turned it to the back page and asked me to read the words aloud. "They will soar on wings like eagles," I read. I could not make out the rest.

"Your great-grandma copied those words," she said. "They held me up through the death of your grandpa. They got me through the Great Depression. They will give you the same strength."

She shut the Bible and gave me a big hug and a wink. Without hesitation, I ran to the attic and retrieved the missing coins. I placed them back in her desk.

I treasure Grandma's Bible. It is one of my most precious possessions. But I cherish even more the memory of Grandma's hug and the words of God she shared that gave me the courage to be honest.

And now, as I read the faded writing, I see a gray-haired woman sitting at the kitchen table with a cup of tea and her tattered old Bible. I have no doubt she is soaring on wings like eagles!

Prayer

Lord, speak to me through Your Word today. Yours are the words of eternal life. In Jesus' name I pray. Amen.

Turning 40

The length of our days is seventy years.
Psalm 90:10

I turned 40 today. Someone said that this milestone puts me somewhere between the age of consent and the state of collapse. I got the usual gag gifts: black balloons, a mug that says "Over the Hill," a bottle of Geritol, and a packet of Depends.

I can hardly imagine that only 40 years ago I was a tiny baby struggling to enter this world full of strange lights and scary voices. In some ways, 40 years seems like an eternity, but suddenly it is just a mere moment in time.

The Israelites wandered in the desert for 40 years before God led them to the Promised Land. I can sympathize with them. Many times I've struggled, searching for my "homeland"—the right husband, the right job, the right church. I didn't trust God to do it for me, so everything took longer.

Turning 40 is almost a relief. If I live until age 80, my life is only half over. It's kind of like getting a clean slate. Please, Lord, help me turn the page and write a great sequel to the first half of my life.

Prayer

Lord, thank You for this day. Help me fill the coming days with joy, hope, and laughter. You have done so much for me. You have made me Your child, You have walked with me through the valley of death and through the mountaintop experiences of life. Stay close beside me through the rest of my life. I trust Your plans for me and ask You to work Your good will in my life. In Jesus' name. Amen.

My Secret Garden

He who dwells in the shelter of the Most High will rest in the shadow of the Almighty. *Psalm 91:1*

My secret garden takes up a small corner in our backyard. I have bird feeders there that the chipmunks also love. They share the sunflower seeds with the sparrows. Assorted pots of geraniums flourish in this secret spot. As do I. When I feel wilted and withered, the secret garden waters my soul. God's creation surrounds my troubled spirit with life. The aroma of roses fills my senses with calm. I watch unusual birds stop to visit. I hear crickets chirp out their cheerful call. I smell a delightful potpourri of lavender and herbs blended together.

Prayer

Lord, thank You for my refuge in this world of concrete. Thank You for this small corner where I can talk to You freely and listen to Your voice, smell Your creation, and see Your beauty. Thank You for my secret garden. In Jesus' name. Amen.

Betty

A friend loves at all times. *Proverbs 17:17*

She dieted with me. She feasted with me. She has cleaned my refrigerator, laughed at my jokes, and listened to my woes. She didn't tell me when my skirt was too tight, but she whispered when I had spinach stuck in my teeth. She didn't ridicule me for my stupid mistakes, and she always put up with my PMS.

She stayed by my side after my husband died. She even played Scrabble with me until 3 a.m. when I was desperate and couldn't sleep. She baby-sat my children when I felt like resigning as a mother. She took the pictures when I remarried.

Together we watched our children grow up. Together we hung a thousand pairs of training pants on the clothesline. Together we planned our children's weddings. Side by side we started solid foods, cheered at ball games, and criticized boyfriends. She supported me when my daughter ran away, and she was the first person I called when my grandson was born.

For more than 20 years she sent me silly cards that arrived just when I needed a lift. She has cried with me. She has laughed with me. She probably knows me better than anyone.

And still she calls me friend.

Prayer

Thanks, Lord, for friends. Amen.

Monday Blues

Let us hold unswervingly to the hope we
profess, for He who promised is faithful.
Hebrews 10:23

Thank You, Lord, for Monday blues—the robin's
egg blue of the sky that frames the warmth of the sun
as it shines down on the earth.

You have replaced the dull, bluish-gray of early
morning with bright, vivid color. On this blue Monday, help me bring brightness to those around me.

Give me an attitude that is a refreshing waterfall
of laughter and hope. Let this attitude infect those
who work with me and whom I serve. Keep the colorful joy of my attitude vivid despite the heat of today's
problems.

Make the words I speak today radiate the warmth
of turquoise. Because of Your love for me, I want to
treat those around me with kindness and honesty. Let
me be a witness to Your presence in my life.

And when I return home this evening and look
into the baby blue eyes of my son, renew my spirit.
Give me the ability to ask about his day and respond
with delight to his new experiences.

As the azure sky melts into midnight blue
evening, remind me on this blue Monday to give You
the thanks. It has truly been a day of wonderful experiences and opportunities to grow as Your servant.
Thank You for the many different shades of color that
You abundantly supply in my life.

Prayer

Father, some people think the color blue is sad. I know it's the color of hope, of the promises You have made and kept. You promised a Messiah, and You sent Your Son, Jesus, to be that promised Savior. You have promised to be with us in all situations and You are. You have promised to bring us safely to You in heaven, and I believe You will. As I go through my day today, help me find ways to work for You. Whether through words or actions, let me be Your witness to family, friends, and customers. Let my faith shine out true blue for You. In Jesus' name. Amen.

The Road Less Traveled

Show me Your ways, O Lord, teach me
Your paths. ... My hope is in You all day
long. *Psalm 25:4–5*

They say I'm crazy to give up this secure job to go out on my own. Some people at work look at me like I'm halfway down the lane to the funny farm. Even my mother questions my decision.

The freeway I have been traveling on is even and smooth. I can see clearly what is ahead. The steady paycheck keeps me going at an even pace. But over the last few years, I feel like an ox pulling a heavy cart, plodding along to the next rest stop. My mundane, boring job makes the load heavier and heavier as I look to the mountain I long to climb.

I have to go. I desperately want to see what's over that mountain. I may fall flat on my face. Rocks and ruts mark the road less traveled, and the first step terrifies me. Can I do it, Lord? Do I have the strength, the tenacity, to make it down the road? I will never know unless I try.

I'm ready to take that step. As I embark down the new road, Lord, guide me over the rough spots. Plant a few signs here and there to keep me on course. Give me the strength to keep going when fear, doubt, and hard times urge me to turn back.

Prayer

Thank You, Lord, for the courage to begin this new journey. With You at my side, I can do anything because with You, all things are possible. In Jesus' name. Amen.

Fasting

After fasting forty days and forty nights, [Jesus] was hungry. *Matthew 4:2*

How did You do it, Lord? I have only fasted 20 hours and I'm weak with hunger. I can't concentrate. When my computer says "main menu," I think of ham and scalloped potatoes. When I see the commercial that says, "Take a bite outta crime," I am more than willing. Right now I could eat my shoelace; it looks a little like licorice.

I now know what the prophets meant when they said their knees were weak with hunger. I am so tired, just lifting my arm is a major ordeal. I try to read to get my mind off eating. I pick up a woman's magazine. It has the latest diet advertised on the front page—right above the picture of chocolate chip fudge cake.

I put down the magazine and decide to read the Bible. "Man does not live by bread alone." Ummm, fresh-baked bread with butter and honey …

But I made a promise to You, Lord, to fast for the full day before Your glorious resurrection. This exercise has given me a whole new respect for You. Again I realize the tremendous sacrifices You made to save me. Please help me to make it these last few hours.

Prayer

I don't think anyone can truly appreciate the sacrifices You made for us, Jesus. This humble effort to say thank You pales by comparison to Your suffering on the cross. Through Your death I have the forgiveness of sins. You have made me right with God. This salvation is a free gift, something I could never hope to repay. Through Your resurrection, which I will celebrate tomorrow, I have the promise of eternal life in heaven. As I eat my Easter breakfast, I will recall the joy of the disciples as they ate with You after Your resurrection. Give me this same joy, and strengthen my faith for the sacrifices I will be called on to make during my life here on earth. In Your saving name I ask this. Amen.

Cleaning House

May there be peace within your walls.
Psalm 122:7

Thank You, God. This has been a good and fruit-ful day. This morning I threw open all the windows, replacing the stale air with freshness and sunshine. I scrubbed the floors and polished the furniture. The windowpanes are clean as crystal. I sent the stacks of magazines to the nursing home. I swept the sidewalks and the back patio.

The house is shining and clean. The cheery fire in the grate warms the cool nip of the fresh autumn air. The old furniture gleams and smells of lemon oil. A pot of vegetable soup simmers on the stove, and the rising rolls are almost ready to pop into the oven.

Prayer

Thank You, God, for the strength to clean. Thank You for the gift of home and furnishings, for the food You sup-ply. Thank You for the ability to maintain this house. Thank You for my senses that take in Your beautiful world. Join my family and me in this place. I trust Your promise to be where two or three gather together. It is good, Lord, to be here. In Jesus' name. Amen.

The Bag Lady in Burger King

Whatever you did for one of the least of these brothers of Mine, you did for Me. Matthew 25:40

After a successful day of Christmas shopping, the car trunk was filled with presents: a sweater for my brother, a fuzzy robe for my mother-in-law, and warm woolen socks for Grandpa. I'd spent more than I'd planned, but Christmas doesn't feel like Christmas without being generous.

On the way home, we stopped at Burger King for a bite to eat. It had stopped snowing and the sky was clearing. It would be a cold night. While munching on fries and sipping hot chocolate, we watched an old woman pull her shopping cart up to the door. Instead of pretty packages, it was filled with garbage bags. She carefully parked the cart close to the building, shuffled inside, and drew a cup of hot water from the urn. She sat by the window where she could watch the cart. She took off the threadbare gloves and wrapped her wrinkled hands around the warm liquid.

We couldn't help staring, but she didn't seem to notice our eyes on her. Or maybe she was used to the glances. Her coat was too ragged and thin for the cold night ahead.

We finished our meals and gathered up the trash: part of an uneaten burger, a few fries, and the dregs of hot chocolate. As we piled into our present-laden car,

I felt the woman looking at me. I turned and saw lonely, lingering, empty eyes.

I wanted to go back inside and hand her $20 for a good meal and a warm bed, but all I had after a day of Christmas shopping were a couple of dollars and an overused credit card.

So I did nothing. And doing nothing is something I will never forget.

Prayer

Lord, I turned my back on You today. I saw someone in need and didn't help, even in some small way. She didn't ask for money or food or shelter, but I could have opened my trunk and given her something warm against the cold night ahead. Her eyes convicted me. You always found time for the people. You healed when You were tired. You taught when You wanted to be alone. You even went to the cross for me. I'm so sorry, Lord. Please forgive me. When I see someone in need, guide me to the best way to help. Remind me always that I am really serving You. In Your name. Amen.

All That Really Matters

Many, O Lord my God, are the wonders You have done. *Psalm 40:5*

Mighty Creator, as I walk beside the river in the cool evening, the promotion doesn't have the same importance in my life as it did this morning. The worry begins to flow gently away, like the golden aspen leaf on the water.

As I watch the geese fly in formation overhead, it doesn't matter as much that my son received a D on his science report. I fall to the back of the flock and ask You to take the lead.

As I sit and watch the deer calmly grazing in the meadow, the unfolded laundry seems as far away as the moon just coming up over the distant horizon.

As I look toward the sunset, the fiery ball casts a warm tangerine glow on the earth. The beauty of Your creation is overwhelming.

Prayer

O Lord my God, heaven and earth are so full of Your glory. My cup truly runneth over. Thank You. Amen.

Looking Back

There is a time for everything, and a season for every activity under heaven. *Ecclesiastes 3:1*

As I thumb through these old journals, it's remarkable how much has changed ... and how much remains the same.

Every year I lament over my need to lose 10, 15, 20 pounds. Every year I discuss problems with the kids and disagreements with my husband. Every year I vow to get out of debt and spend more time in prayer. I long for peace in my life. I vow to do better at work, quit gossiping, and write more letters.

Every year the beauty of the first snow, peace roses, new colts, and autumn leaves astound me. I drink in the radiance of a sunset and laugh at babies' toes. Each spring I feel a rebirth and each fall I get a little melancholy.

I read about the prayers that were answered—and those that haven't been answered yet. Every time I was sure that I could not take one more crisis, Your strength, Lord, helped me tackle another challenge. My daughter ran away, but she came home. My husband lost his job but another followed. We got sick; we got well. We fought against each other and fought together.

There were moments when I thought You had deserted me, Father, and moments I felt You whispering in my ear. Looking back through the pages, I see the days You carried me, scolded me, pushed me, and comforted me. You are always here for me.

Prayer

Lord, thank You for these diaries. In looking back, I find the faith to keep looking forward. Keep me always in Your protective care. Thank You for the faith that keeps me going. Thank You for making me Your child. Thank You for another year as Your servant here on earth. In Jesus' name. Amen.